Buffalo Children

How I Became a Buffalo Mother

By Carol Klein

Chapter 1   Why Buffalo? Why us?

When people learn that we raise buffalo, they have lots of questions. After "How many?" and "Where do you live?" usually comes the big one; "Why buffalo?" Somewhere in that question lurks a sneaking suspicion as to our good sense, if not our sanity. We had heard that suspicion before in the voices of our friends in California when we announced that we were moving to Missouri. Perplexed, "Missouri? Why Missouri?" they would ask.

This is a story about our new herd of American Bison which we prefer to call buffalo. To us, all the magic, history, and wonder of these magnificent animals is summed up in the one word, BUFFALO.

Decisions about the care and happiness of our little herd – 31 animals at this moment, is our responsibility and our pleasure. That's why telling you a little bit about us seemed a logical place to start the story. It will also give you a chance to make your own judgment about our mental state for having embarked on this adventure. I guess I should warn you from the start that Leon was 70 years old when we got the first buffalo, and that neither of us had any experience with any kind of cattle.

I was born Carol Sue Shivers in Florida back in 1944. My loving parents raised me, along with and older sister and two younger brothers on a chicken farm. We had roughly 20,000 chickens laying eggs every day of the year. It was our job to gather, wash, sort and pack those eggs.

Leon was born Leon Edgar Klein in Southern California in 1924. His youth was spent terrorizing the Santa Monica Bay area along with his buddies Frank and Jack. Tormenting little sister Jean was another favorite pastime of the trio.

Before I had even learned to speak, Leon had gone to Europe to help win "the big one", WW2. In February of 1945, the B17 Flying Fortress he was in was shot down over Munich, Germany. He was a POW for the remaining months of the war until Patton's 3rd Army came by to liberate them. Thank you, Patton's 3rd Army and the American Red Cross.

While I was busy growing up with all those chickens and eggs, Leon was terrorizing southern California again, this time subcontracting light weight cement and plaster. In 1965, construction was in the dumps and Leon was out of work. Maybe Leon's good sense was in question back then also, because he decided it was time for him to become a crop duster. He moseyed on down to Marigold, MS to a crop dusting school.

When I showed up on the scene in Santa Monica a few months later, he was all set to try out his new career.

Having recently graduated from Florida State University with a degree in Health Education, I set out for California that year. I landed a job as a social worker for the L.A. County Social Services, just like Leon's mother as it turned out. Leon took me up in his AT6 fighter plane on our first date. Being upside down and backwards at 200 mph over Los Angeles at night could have had a permanent affect on my brain. If there's a screw lose, I could probably blame him. That was 28 years ago, and he hasn't been able to get rid of me yet.

When the FAA gave Leon a recommendation for his first crop dusting job, everyone figured it was the only way the feds could get him out of the Santa Monica Airport. He was off to the little town of Lovelock, NV to "fly for pay the way he would otherwise have been arrested for flying". Would you believe, Lovelock had just lost its one and only social worker. When I applied for the job, I was tested, interviewed and hired in less than an hour.

Leon soon sold his fighter plane and bought a crop duster plane. It was a big Stearman bi-plane with a 600 hp radial engine. The bad part was the very short growing season in Nevada, only 3 months work for him each year.

We were married there in Lovelock back in 1967. Cost of living was high and pay was low, so after 15 months we decided to return to "civilization" in LA. Leon had really enjoyed his summers as a crop duster, but had gotten it more or less out of his system.

I began teaching for the Los Angeles City Schools. Leon went back to college and also gave flying lessons. After his AA degree, he went to law school for a year. Then for a couple of years he was a field investigator for the Plaster's Union Trust Fund. Finally he came full circle back to plaster contractor.

Having sold his crop duster Stearman, Leon bought a Piper PA12. Later he changed to a Bonanza, then an L13, a Citabria, an Apache twin, then a Cessna 180. I may have forgotten a few along the way. There was no doubt about it, he was a certified "airport bum". At least I always knew where to find him.

Next thing I knew, I had been teaching for 13 years. It was time for a change. Some of our flying buddies moved down to San Diego, and that seemed like a good move for us also. We found the perfect house at the end of a quiet canyon in Lakeside. Neither Leon nor I was working. Guess we were just not ready for retirement though. We spent a lot of time playing in Mexico, gardening at home and stuff like that.

In 2 years we were gradually going batty and broke at the same time. We needed something to do and a way to supplement our retirement income. One thing led to another. We found ourselves in a woodworking business in our garage. We were supplying wooden cutouts to crafters and craft stores though out Southern California. Before long we were shipping products by UPS all over the country. We were also out growing our garage.

We looked all over the western states for a place to move to and weren't having much luck. Then a friend suggested we check out Missouri. It seemed like a long shot. But airfares were low and a trip sounded good.

We arrived in the Ozarks in the middle of May. Beautiful all year round, the Ozarks are at their best in May. We found heaven just north of the Arkansas state line, near the small town of Jane, MO just three days after our arrival. We both knew it was perfect the moment we laid our eyes on the farm. The large, almost new country home set right in the middle of 40 acres of fields and some woods. The view was breath taking. Hills rolled out in every direction as far as the eyes could see. Trees and meadows decorated the hills in an unending quilt of green.

Leon even thought he could land an airplane in the back yard. We bought our new home that very day. Neither of us have had the slightest flicker of regret for the move. Going back to California - or anywhere else for that matter – would be unthinkable. This is HOME for us, forever.

The farm is so beautiful that it was all we could hope for. Never did we expect it to be improved on but the buffalo have done just that. Its not only more beautiful, the buffalo have made it so much more interesting to live here.

We needed a place to do our woodworking, so we had a building put up near the house before we moved. The new shop worked out just right. It has lots of room and was heated and air conditioned like a cocoon. Business kept growing. Soon we were shipping our little wooden cutouts to distributors in Canada and Japan as well. We built a cabin by a lake 40 miles away as a weekend "get away". We rarely have the time or inclination anymore to get away to it very often.

Leon bought a Super Cub airplane as he knew his back yard strip would not be very long. One flight over the property proved even the Super Cub would be too marginal for that landing strip. He sold the plane and hung up his wings for good. There was plenty of other mischief for him to get into around here.

You've gotten a pretty good picture of "Why Missouri?" is the place for us. Now to the good stuff. "Why Buffalo?" I mentioned that our home sits in the middle of a 40 acre pasture. It is picture perfect. Unfortunately, it won't stay that way by itself. It needs animals to graze and tractors to mow hay and cut brush. Dairy and beef cattle surrounds the farm, and horses. We just couldn't work up any enthusiasm for raising a few head of cattle on our little place. Forty acres had seemed like a real "spread" to city slickers like us. By farm standards, it really is quite small.

When we would head out to our "get away" cabin on the lake, we would pass by a farm that raised buffalo. It was the high point of the drive. Sometimes we would pull off the road and watch the animals for awhile. An idea just kind of spouted up out of nowhere. Neither of us can remember exactly when. Why couldn't we have buffalo like that? Why indeed?

We had already established that a few head of cattle would not make us much money. Buffalo could probably make us that much as a tax write off. Now there was an idea that appealed to Leon. While we don't make all that much money with our woodworking, Leon hates to pay taxes. You don't think I snookered him with that idea, do you?

That was how it started. It became my goal in life to find out everything there was to know about buffalo. Funny thing, though, one of the first things I learned about buffalo was that you could actually make money raising them. So much for tax write offs. But making money would be OK too.

The real truth "why buffalo?" is that we love them. From the moment we first laid eyes on them, they stole our hearts. Now here they were, coming to live with us and helping to support us though our seasoned years. It was the perfect addition to our little piece of paradise.

There are so many things that make buffalo special. I could hardly begin to describe to you in this short space. Here's just a few to wet your appetite.

Buffalo taste great and are good for you. How could you say that? Eat one? Actually eat one of those magnificent animals? Yes! Definitely!. Its really the nature of things. We eat meat every day, don't we my fellow Americans? And buffalo is low in calories and cholesterol. It has no chemicals or hormones added to it. Because it has so little fat, it is cooked differently. In flavor, it rivals... and often surpasses.... even the finest beef. By eating buffalo, we help guarantee their survival. Because raising buffalo for meat is profitable, more people will want to raise buffalo – so there will be more buffalo. It works!

The better you know buffalo, the more you will love them. They are wonderful, wild things. You can't make them do anything they don't want to do. The power of their bodies is amazing. They can out run race horses and out maneuver the best of cow ponies. Fences can't stop them if they want out. A bull could jump a 6 foot fence from a standstill, but he'd probably just go through it. They are very protective of their own and you don't want to mess with them if you don't have to.

But they come up to the fence and stick out their long tongues in a silent request for treats. Their big dark eyes watch everything and seem to communicate a wisdom beyond expression. They trust me. I am their friend and they are mine. Each one has a personality of its own and I never tire of watching them. I'm sure glad they are here.

There were millions of buffalo ranging across this country in peace when the "white man" came here. By the year 1900, there were fewer than 1000 buffalo left in the world. A few handful of people were responsible for preventing their extinction. Now their numbers are rising dramatically. There are roughly 300,000 buffalo in the U.S. today.

Here's hoping they will return to their position of dominance in this country once more. The world will be so much richer with them in it!

Chapter 2 The Buffalo Are Coming. Ready or Not?

Once the decision had been made to raise buffalo, the adventure began. We needed to find buffalo to bring here. And we needed to be good and ready for them when they arrived. It was just the kind of challenge I enjoyed, a research project with a real goal.

A stop to visit the buffalo herd owners near the lake proved unfruitful. Maybe they had too many people pestering them, being on the highway like that. My inquiries did not receive a serious response. He suggested the Butterfield Ranch, but didn't know where it was. It was a start.

I called the county extension agent. He referred me to the State Extension Service. They sent me some reference materials and gave me two important phone numbers.

The first was to the American Bison Association in Denver, Colorado. We immediately became members of that organization. Their Bison Breeders Handbook contained just the kind of advice we needed to prepare for our new herd. Their bi-monthly magazine called "Bison World" also brought fresh information and enjoyment.

The Bison Breeders Handbook convinced us that calves would definitely be the animals to start with. They would adjust to their new surroundings. As long as they have food, water and other buffalo to live with, they would be inclined to stay put. Since fences aren't very good at keeping in an unhappy buffalo, we wanted them to be unconditionally satisfied with their new home.

The second phone number brought me to Alyce Knoth in Kansas City. A widowed lady, Alyce no longer actually raised buffalo. But her enthusiasm and knowledge of the animals and for the ABA was contagious. She also had the phone number of the Butterfield Ranch.

Larry and Kay Butterfield lived out in Beloit, Kansas, about a day's drive away.   Yes, they did have buffalo calves for sale. Would we like to come out for a visit? We didn't need a second invitation. At their ranch, the Kansas prairie was rich in grass and buffalo babies. What cute little critters they were. Only a month or two old, they were orange rather than brown like their mothers. Some were tagging along side their mothers, but most were playing together in small groups while their mothers grazed near by.

I could have scooped dozens of them up and wished them home with me. But their mothers were another story. They were huge and had very serious horns. It was rather intimidating to picture them in my back yard. Lets start with calves!

Larry explained that all his calves would be sold by the end of summer. However, they would not be weaned from their mothers until late fall. At that time, the heifer calves would be calfhood vaccinated and all would be ear tagged. The babies would then be available for delivery to their adoptive homes. Talk about good timing! We got there in time to buy calves, but would have a full six months to prepare for them. It was perfect.

Leon had already been busy. He was looking for a tractor at auctions, etc. The local Belarus Tractor dealer turned out to be the best deal. For roughly $20,000 he could get a 65 HP tractor complete with enclosed cab, post hole digger, front end loader and bale spear. Our bank would be delighted to finance it for us. I knew he would appreciate the heater and air conditioning.

Our neighbor, Jack Johnson, had agreed to hay our field for us on shares. There were something like 130 big bales of hay rolled up in the field. More than 50 of them would be a waste for us. Leon sure had fun gathering them up with his tractor. He would scoop a bale up without even slowing down. He took them to a storage area near the corral. That done, he continued spearing Jack's bales and placing them in rows. Jack could now easily load them on his big trailer and run home with them. We had our babies winter menu on hand.

The tractor came in real handy for fencing as well. The bucket pushed down little trees along the fence line. The two young men working on the fence would use it to pile up the brush and trees that they cut. The post hole digger got lots of exercise as well. Soon you could drive all the way around our fence line.

Extra strands of barbed wire were added to the top of the fence, making it roughly six feet high. That required eight foot metal T-posts to be added frequently along the fence. Metal twisted fence stays attached the new wire to the existing fence in between the posts. The results were very satisfying. Our fence was not only taller than before, it was stronger. While Tim and Clint worked though the heat, rain, chiggers and poison ivy on the fence, Leon and I earned their wages making wooden cutouts in our air conditioned shop. That was a good deal for us.

We needed a corral. It would house the calves for a few weeks when they first arrive so they can settle down and get acquainted with their new surroundings. Later it would be used for weaning calves and vaccinations, etc. We discovered a great company making portable corrals just ten miles away. They had exceptionally tall and strong panels available at good prices. We also chose a circular sweep and a super duty squeeze chute.

A crash cage would have to be added to the front of the squeeze chute. Buffalo are too fast to catch in a traditional head gate the way cattle are. So they have to crash into a cage in front of the chute to stop them. Then the head gate can catch therm around the neck. Sibley promised to make us a crash cage if we weren't in too much of a hurry. Its not here yet in picture below.

There were two factors taken into account when we decided on a "portable" corral. We didn't know much about corrals or working buffalo. It would allow us to make changes as we went along. Also, in the event we found buffalo too much for us, we could always sell the corral. Well, at this point, you never really know. We could be getting in over our heads!

OK, babies, we're ready for you. The Butterfields had suggested we come to the Kansas Buffalo Association Auction in November in Salinas, Kansas. Alyce Knoth asked if we could help man the NBA booth at the American Royal in Kansas City a few days before that. Off we went to combine both events into one trip.

At the American Royal, we met Wayne Copp. He invited us to stop by and see his herd and watch the animals being loaded into trailers. Wayne's ranch was truly an education. We went on to the auction, had a great time and made new friends....... But we didn't buy animals. Ours should be coming anytime now from the Butterfield Ranch.

Leon's lifelong buddies, Frank and Jack, showed up in November to help Leon celebrate his 70th birthday. We were hoping the buffalo would arrive before Frank and Jack left. They didn't. Marshall did show up to make a new pond in front of the house.

We found a 1989 Ford 350 pickup truck. The red paint was like new. It had an extended cab and duelies. Only 43,000 miles and $11,500. That was the truck we wanted! Later we would need a stock trailer to complete the outfit. Still the buffalo didn't come.

As 1994 was drawing to a close, everyone was asking what happened to the buffalo? Leon joked that he had to cover his head and sneak down the hollow these days. I started calling Larry Butterfield each week. But the weather and other things were not co-operating out in Kansas. The babes were still with their mothers. Then Larry had a suggestion for us. We could get the buffalo from his friend and partner, Dr. Kendricks. Those buffalo were weaned back in December and were less than an hours drive away.

A call to Kr. Kendricks confirmed the new plan. We could get 12 heifer calves for the contracted price of $1,200 and we could get an extra three calves for $1400 each if we wanted. We wanted. He could deliver them Friday, if that would be OK. It was.

For nine months we had been planning, dreaming and working. On Friday those dreams would come true. We were ready. We were more than ready.

Chapter 3   Friday the 13th They're Here!

Friday the 13th didn't exactly dawn. It poured right out of a cold January sky. Bucket of rain were falling. How could this happen? Another day without our buffalo. Oh, heartbreak again!

The telephone startled me when it rang at about 8:30 a.m. Could it be? Yes! Dr. Kendrick's voice on the other end of the phone announced that they were all loaded and he was heading our way. They were really coming! Now! Its a wonder I didn't run in circles for the next hour.

Leon and I stood in the cold rain with huge smiles on our faces as Dr. Kendricks' trailer backed up to the red corral gate. He opened the trailer door and out charged 15 adorable, wet, frightened buffalo babies. I wanted to hug them all. They huddled with their little butts together and their tiny horns facing the world. No problem, they would soon know that I was their new mother.

Wet and bedraggled, but not cold. It has to be well below zero for them to feel the cold. Buffalo are well insulated.

The grassy corral that had welcomed its new tenants soon turned into a giant mud pie. Even though we had placed the corral on our highest ground, there were inches of mud for our buffalo to stand in. The rain had barely let up for a few days when the snow came. Six inches of beautiful powder fell overnight. It stayed on the ground for a couple of days, then melted right into that big mud hole.

No kind of weather could have kept me away from that pen. I would perch up on a seven foot high rung of the corral and visit with the babies for hours. Twenty degree weather with a wind chill of below zero, those critters kept my heart so warm I didn't even notice. They were getting used to me and the sound of my voice.

We planned to keep the buffalo in the corral for at least two, possibly three weeks. It was important for them to adjust to us and to their new home. Word was out in the neighborhood of their arrival. Coated with mud and looking bedraggled, they evoked more sympathy than admiration from their audiences. Shouldn't we let them out now? But we held firm.

Leon used his new tractor to dump a large bale of hay over the fence into a different part of the corral every few days. I would steal into the corral with the babies and scatter the remains of the old bale over the mud. Gradually, the mud was covered with hay.

We also carried buckets of grain to their feeders each day and set up chairs outside their pen. It was more comfortable for us and the buffalo were less intimidated by sitting figures. Curiosity was getting the best of them. We would toss them sweet molasses range cubes, each time a little closer to our feet. We had been holding out treats to them for days with no takers. Then, finally, one brave little nose came closer and closer. It didn't grab the cube, but sniffed the fingers that held the food. Finally, the mouth opened and a pink and brown tongue curled around the cube. That curious, brave little buffalo had a tag in her ear with the #13 on it. We would call that girl Friday, Friday the 13th. Good Friday. Thirteen always was my lucky number.

Now I had to find names for the other girls. Buffalo generally live for 20 to 30 years. These would live here in our yard for pretty much the rest of their lives and ours too. We would be family and each one of them would be very precious to us. Ear tag #1 belonged to a large shy girl with a broken tip on one of her horns. Being the 'first' lady, I would call her Eve. Eve was to eventually become the dominant female in our little herd. Eve's friend Echo had ear tag #2. She was also large and shy and not overly curious.

A medium sized, wild little girl wore tag #3. When Leon brought them a new bale of hay, she wold butt it and kick it and try to climb it. She had a lot of spirit. I would call her Mariah, after the wind.

I smiled at the beautiful little girl wearing ear tag #9. That was easy. She would be Chanel #9. The girl wearing #11 seemed like Josie to me, short for Josephine. Ginger wore #18. The name suited her.

I named #21 Blackjack. But I was soon calling her Lady Jacqueline. She was large, beautiful, and elegant. She didn't need to push others around. She would just walk up and take her rightful position. She had class.

The little girl wearing #22 became Rachael. She was named after my four year old great niece who was soon to move nearby. And Rosie, she was a sweet girl wearing #26. She was nice to everyone, even solo. Solo was #27. She was blind n one eye and always stayed by herself.

When our neighbor, Juna, came to visit the buffalo, #46 took an instant liking to her. Soon Juna was feeding her cubes even though she had never eaten from our hands. We named her Margie, after Juna's daughter. It was a good family name for me too, as my mother and sister are both Margie. We called #39 June.

We live in Jane, MO and I have a good friend named Janie. #47 seemed like a plain Jane, so she won that name. Janie proved to be the 'Ugly Duckling" because she blossomed into the most beautiful buffalo girl of all.

Finally, there was little Dulce, #48. She was the baby, with just nibbens of horns showing. What a sweet little baby. But the buffalo girls spoiled her rotten and let her get away with anything. You should have seen her at feeding time. She would go over, under or through the line of girls at the feeder to get more than her share of grain. Three weeks had gone by, the girls all had their names and had settled down very nicely. They knew us and they could always find water here in the corral. The big day had come. It was time to let them out.

Months earlier, I had tied yellow plastic ribbons all along the fences. It was more than an welcome, it was a traffic sign. I had been told that when you first turn them loose in an new place that they would run. I didn't want them running through a fence and disappearing.

Leon's buddy, Junior, was on hand with us to watch the girls' reaction to their freedom. Leon opened the gate. Nothing happened. The girls walked to the opening and stopped. Taking a bucket of range cubes to the opening, Leon held one out to the girls. They craned their necks out to reach his hand. Finally one girl stepped out, then another. A few range cubes were eaten before one of the girls got the message. Freedom!

Within seconds the charge was on. Down the wide alley they went and through the gate into the large back pasture. Next they swung to the west and out of sight behind some trees. We held our breath. Would they see the fence and turn? Back into sight they sped, heading along that fence now going north.

So far, so good! Another fence was coming up. It was time to turn. I said turn! Crash! It was a sickening sound. There was a pause and confusion in the ranks. Once more the little herd picked up speed and headed east along our side of the fence. Past the pond, around the trees, back around the pond and on and on they ran. Finally they ran out of steam. Coming to a stop, they began munching on the tall grass. It was their first grass in weeks. They were happy kids.

Once they settled down, we jumped into the car to check out the damaged fence. The metal posts were bent, but the strands of wire had held. The yellow ribbons were gone, seems the curious horses in the neighbor's pasture had pulled them off.

That evening, the girls showed up back at the corral looking for grain for dinner. Margie was sporting a rather large scrap across the tip of her nose. Guess we know who found that back fence first.

Serenity spread across the field. Our buffalo are here, home at last.

Meeting the neighbors

Chapter 4   Buffalo Plucking: How the Vest Was Made

Spring had come to the Ozark hills. Graceful white Dogwoods and airy white Savis contrasted with the fresh bright green of new leaves and the indescribably beautiful roseberry petals of Redbud trees. Wildflowers bloomed and faded, but were replaced with ever more beautiful varieties. When the blackberries bloomed, it was now or never for old man winter. Sometimes a late last frost or "Blackberry Winter" would take a nip out of spring. It didn't this year.

The buffalo girls never seemed to mind the winter cold. Frost on their backs and steam bellowing out of their mouths made quite a sight on winter mornings. Now that spring was here, they seemed to be getting lively and energetic. Just about every day now, we would see them running around the fields. I called it bonging. They have a rather strange gait that reminds me of children skipping. They look very happy and like they are having lots of fun.

When one buffalo runs, they all do. It's hard for some of them to keep up. Sometimes

the leaders find themselves running alone, as the group behind them veers off is another direction. The first leaders then have to run even harder to catch up with the group. More often that not the end their run is in one of the ponds. When the buffalo start running, all other activities at the house stop so we can watch the show.

The girls were ready to shed those beautiful winter coats they had been wearing and many days were down right warm now. After a nice long run and a dip in the pond. A quiet nap in the sun was in order. Soon I began finding little tufts of fur on the barb wire, sticking to a girl's horn or hanging off a tree. It was incredibly soft. This was their 'baby hair', their first wool. I learned that buffalo have eight times more hair follicles than cows do. Their hair was longer on some parts of their body, like the head and hump, than it was on their sides.

Now I would see patches of hair loosening on their wool. But when I reached out to 'pluck' it, that girl would quickly move out of reach. If I happened to be successful, a shiver would run across their whole body when the hair came off. I also learned very quickly that a reflex kick often accompanied an unconsentual touch. Believe me, those girls could kick in any direction, hard and fast. Surprise was not going to be the key to successful 'buffalo plucking'.

There was a big soft fuzzy wad of buffalo hair in my jeans pocket by now. I was enthralled with it. I had visions of having it spun and knitted into the most wonderful garments. I had no idea how much buffalo wool it would take to make anything with, or how much I could collect. I decided to shoot for a vest. It would be more versatile than a sweater and require less wool. Now I needed a plan and a method of gathering the wool. I decided on a shot gun approach. Any and every way I could get it.

One technique for collecting wool proved to be both fun and profitable. I would hold out a range cube with one hand while reaching for a tuft of wool with the other. Those girls wanted those range cubes really bad. They were practically wall-eyed trying to keep watch on both my hands at the same time. I won at least half the times.

The bulges of wool in my pockets would grow each day. I started to fill a large plastic bag with my bounty. But now the easier wool to reach had been plucked from their heads and shoulders, and plucking became definitely more of a challenge. Their horns had grown quite long by now. Caution was always needed to avoid them. It made the game a little more exciting. Buffalo plucking isn't as dangerous as it might sound. It was always done through corral bars or at least a fence.

Some of the girls would never let me pluck even a least little bit of their wool. I didn't think that was very nice of them. On the other hand, one girl seemed to enjoy being plucked. Chanel, ear tag #9, was more than happy to trade plucks for range cubes. She would even let me pluck her for free. Soon she was bare from one end to the other of any shreds of her winter coat. Her new short rich hair gave way to bare brown skin on her rump.

Those other girls who wouldn't let me pluck them were starting to look a little scrappy by now. Hair was hanging in long hunks from their heads and sides. I sure eyed those locks enviously.

It was time for plan two. The girls would rub up against special trees to get rid of that pesky wool. Weeds and twigs would snatch it off their sides. When they came to the corral for grain, pieces would be left on the ground. Tufts would be left behind where they napped in the grass. Easter egg hunts were never so much fun. I found myself spending more and more time searching the nooks and crannies of our property for those precious scraps of wool. One plastic bag was full, then another.

We bought a 4-wheeler off road bike this spring. It make my search much easier and a lot more enjoyable – and safer too. I did have one problem, no actually two. First there was this awful thorny vine with the beautiful name Greenbriar. It had a real unfortunate habit of snagging me all the time and covering my arms and legs with scratched.

The other problem was even worse. Ticks were now in season. You could usually feel the big ones crawling on you and dispatch them before they had a chance to bite. But those tinsey, tiny little seed ticks were something else. You couldn't even see them, but their bite was as vicious as the big guys. You'd itch for a week from every little bite. Needless to say, a bath and change of clothes was called for after every safari. Thank goodness the chiggers don't come out until the forth of July. The buffalo plucking was all over by then.

Scissortail Flycatcher in my pasture

Buffalo wool was not the only thing I was searching for. I needed someone to spin and knit this treasure. I heard about Edwidge at the **Scissortail Gallery** in Bartlesville, OK, a hundred or so miles away. Her friendly voice on the phone was encouraging. Yes, she would be delighted to spin my buffalo wool, and she had a friend who could weave it into a vest for me. Eureka! This was it! If I could mail her a small piece, she would spin a sample.

Edwidge called back, excited, when she received the sample. It was much softer than other buffalo wool she had spun and cleaner as well. Soft probably because it was the first 'baby wool', but maybe because it had been hand plucked. Still, you wouldn't want to stick your nose into that bag of wool. It had a definite buffalo aroma.

Should I wash the wool before I ship it to her/ Yes, that would be nice was her reply. I was going to put it in a pillow case and throw it in the washer on a gentle cycle if that would work. NO! NO! NO! Came a horrified reply. If you agitate the wool in warm soapy water, it will break into pieces and stick together to become felt. I didn't know that! It could become unusable. That was close! It pays to ask questions.

Edwidge suggested I wash it by hand in the sink, rinsing it until the water ran clear. It took a lot of rinses. Next, pat it gently with towels. Then lay it out on towels to dry. So I cleared an eight foot table in my workroom under the ceiling fan, covered the table with towels and spread out the little wet tufts of wool.

I was surprised the next morning to find the pile of wool had grown. As it dried, it fluffed and fluffed. I picked out the driest pieces and put them in a box. But the 'buffalo' on the table continued to grow. It looked a lot like Chanel #9. I had no idea I had collected so much wool from our girls. I shipped it off to Edwidge along with a vest to use as a pattern. Then I waited with a pleasurable anticipation. It was fall before the final call came in. The vest was finished.

I wasted little time getting over to Bartlesville. The vest was, well, plain. Brown and plain. Anticipating this, I brought along some antler buttons and buffalo teeth as possible decorations. We played with possibilities, but they didn't seem to work. All the way home I plotted and plotted. Leon thought the vest was real plain...

We were leaving the following day for a buffalo auction in Oklahoma. There would be a buyers' social. Our friends, Mike and Janie from Horseshoe Mountain would be there. I wanted to wear my precious vest. I finally settled for sewing hunks of raw wool on the front of the vest and decorating them with teeth and small gold beads. It was an interesting accent. Ladies at the buyers' social would look at the teeth and wool. When they herd that the cloth was woven from our buffalo babies wool, they had to touch it. Then they told others who would come and check it out. I was proud of my plain brown vest. It was a very, very precious garment. It keeps me close to my buffalo girls.

Buffalo wool and leather can be made into wonderful clothing
These designs are by Ruth Huffman

Chapter 5 Chanel and the Flies

Faded petals were falling from the blackberry vines. Hard, green little berries in their shadow promised summer was soon to follow, warm and sweet. Spring rain fell, sometimes gentle and soft, more often in pelting torrents. Grass was growing taller. My eyes were beginning to itch. Hay season had arrived.

God must have been a sports fan. He devised a magnificent contest for spring. The scrimmage would take place in the fields, with huge rolls of grass as the prize. The players were the farmers with their tractors of every size, age, make and color. Their opponents would be the sun and rain, determined to keep the grass in tact as a gift to Mother Earth.

In mid May, the grass would send out a bud wrapped in a sheath of grass called a 'boot'. This was the signal for the contest to begin. An eager farmer would venture into his field, his mower following the tractor like a faithful shadow. Pale rows of grass lay drying in the sun. If successful, this farmer would have a very rich prize.

At this stage of growth, the grass was brimming with protein and energy, captured for use in the dark, cold days of winter. However, it would not have the volume of a later cut. But then, he just might manage to sneak in a second cutting, a real prize. Who knows, he could even dream of a third cutting. It sometimes happens.

Other farmers prepared for the contest. Soon fields were humming with equipment. The first fields were stirred and fluffed and the grass raked into neat rows for the baler. The skies clouded over. There was a frantic rush below. Big droplets splattered across the fields. Round one for the rain.

Satisfaction showed on the faces of those who had not played that round. They had guessed right for once. When the rain stopped, the cut grass would have to be stirred again, and dried and raked, hopefully before another shower caught them still in the field. No major harm was done, just extra work and a small loss in quality, plus time and expense.

If you are a farmer, you must play the game. Gradually the winning players were collecting their prize. Bales were being hauled into barns and down the highways, or stacked into large rows at the edge of the field. Still the rains came often and hard. Creeks were full and the ground saturated. Three inches of rain in one afternoon sent creeks flooding over their banks, causing havoc along their course. Lakes and ponds filled and dam spillovers sent the water on down the line. Would the rain never let up?

Finally the skies turned blue for good and the fields dried and the grass grew. Then the fields were dry. The grass stopped growing. Even weeds were beginning to wilt. We could use some rain. Dust began to blow. Farmers watched the grass wither and wondered if they would have to feed some of their precious hay this summer. We need rain, need it bad.

Not to brag, but we have an excellent hay field. Our neighbor had a larger baler this year. It not only made larger bales, but tied them tighter. There would be less waste. He took nearly 100 of these larger bales off our 20 acre field. We kept only thirty for ourselves as we still had lots left over from last year. Why waste the hay? There was so much grass left on the ground, it would be a long time before we would have to feed any hay.

Leon enjoyed the hay season and helped out when the big round bales were ready to be removed from the fields. Unfortunately when the day was through, no one went back to shut the gate – the girls were free to roam. When we went outside the next morning, there were 'buffalo chips' all over the yard where the girls had pooped. It was a shock! Where were our girls? Why right where they were supposed to be, in the pasture. They had gone back home to the pasture where the grazing was better. Or maybe the dogs had scared them, causing them to go back. However it happened we were very lucky. They could have been miles away by now and how would we have gotten them back? It was a sobering thought and a strong reminder of our responsibilities.

We had a lot to learn about raising bison. Experienced ranchers told us to forget everything we knew about raising cattle – bison are different. We felt we were ahead of the game because we didn't know anything to forget. We knew nothing about raising cattle either. We had also been told that bison were really hearty animals and had very little illness for us to worry about. Right.

I was standing at the fence visiting with the little herd when I noticed they all had the 'runs'. Their poop was like water and was that coughing I heard? Yes, someone definitely sounded like they had a serious cough. Oh, I heard another one. They're sick. Oh, NO! I quickly placed a call to Dr. Kendricks to ask his advice.

Dr Kendricks listened closely and told me he didn't know about the cough. If it continued or got worse or spread to other animals then I should get the veterinarian out. But he had good news about the runny manure. Seems the tender grass in the spring had less fiber. It was digested fast and went through their system without the bulk hay had produced. Runny manure was perfectly natural in the spring. It wouldn't hurt to put out a mineral with extra magnesium in it this time of year but there was nothing to worry about.

I was excited to share the information I had learned with my friend Janie. We were learning together about bison and talked almost every day. When Janie learned about the naturalness of 'runny poop' in the spring, she could not thank me enough for letting her know. She had gotten so worried about the problem in her herd that they were thinking about draining their pond. Yup, we had lots to learn. We were later to learn that the 'runny poop' could also be a symptom of a really serious problem in bison, intestinal parasites, but for now we were in the clear.

With the heat of summer, both the buffalo girls and I were enjoying a special treat.... watermelon. I cut up watermelon rind one day just to see if my girls would like it. They loved it! From then on melon was a sweeter pleasure for me. When the buffalo girls 'planted' their own melons, I saved some of the seeds. Next year I would try giving them a helping hand planting their melon patch. Eve was crazy over the melon. It changed her whole personality. She became the most aggressive and dominant girl in the herd. She wanted all the melon.

The "mud pie' of a corral had turned into a dust bowl. The girls still came there each day for their fifty pounds of grain. That is about three pounds each. We knew it was not necessary, but it didn't hurt any. There were minerals and vitamins added to the grain and we wanted to make sure they wouldn't be lacking in any nutrients. They were looking great.

On a closer look, we noticed that the buffalo girls were each being accompanied by their own personal herds, or hoards, of flies. There were little flies, big flies and biting flies. They swarmed on the girls backs and stomachs and all around their eyes. Nasty! Nasty! We have to do something about that.

A trip to the feed store brought us a few weapons to defeat the flies. There was stuff to put in their feed. It wouldn't affect the girls, but would prevent the development of fly larva in the 'buffalo chips'. There was stuff for them to rub against. Also a spray. We'll try them all.

The girls were not aware of the addition to their feed or the special benefits of the rub. Leon put the spray in a big garden sprayer and showered them when they came to dinner. They squealed and ran around like teenage girls. It did seem to help, for a few days at a time. It was a never ending battle. The flies always came back.

The long summer evenings were a special time. I would ride the ATV after dinner in the pasture with the dogs, two golden retrievers. When the dogs tired of running, they were delighted to ride with me. Sugar would lie across the luggage rack behind me. Amigo rode between my arms with his front feet on the handlebars. They enjoyed the ride as much as I did.

The dogs would have to get off before I would stop and visit with the buffalo girls. They didn't get excited about my presence unless I had food. This was a social call, not mealtime. They treated me as one of their own. Gradually girls would drift up to greet me with a touch of their nose, then drift on by to graze. It was Chanel's turn to say hello. I was horrified! Her eye was totally white and blind. There were flies and goop dripping and she rubbed it against the rack of the bike. It was obviously hurting or itching badly.

I checked on the other girls. There were a lot of eye flies. There was watering and white secretions. But Chanel was the only one with damaged eyes. My mind was telling me this was the "pink eye' I had read about in the Bison Breeders Handbook. I hurried back to the house to consult those references. It sure seemed like "pink eye". Please don't let Chanel be blind like Solo!

First thing in the morning, I had the Veterinarian on the phone. We had not needed a Vet before for the buffalo girls. Dr. France was about fifteen miles away. He had been their "family doctor" when they were still in Dr. Kendicks herd. His name was on their health certificates, since he had given them their official calfhood vaccinations. He was also well liked in the neighborhood, especially for treating horses. I had checked all this out beforehand, but never had a need to contact him until now. He was very nice and would be out in a few hours. He said it could be an injury, he would have to check her out.

When Dr. France arrived, the girls were waiting in the shade near the driveway. Chanel came to the fence for a treat and he could easily inspect her eye. My fears were confirmed, pink eye. The Breeders Handbook talked about the best treatment, being a shot of antibiotics under the eyelid, or sewing the eye shut or gluing on an eye patch.

Our squeeze chute was not operational. We still had no crash cage on the front. Besides, I could just visualize chasing all fifteen girls through the chute in order to catch Chanel. The trauma would be unimaginable. Tranquilizing Chanel seemed to be a much better plan, although not without danger.

As Chanel stretched her nose through the fence for a treat, Dr. France jabbed her with a syringe on a long stick. I don't think she even realized what had happened. It took ten minutes or more for the medicine to begin taking hold. Our friend Joe Hart showed up about then. Joe had been at Dr France's office and had heard he would be treating one of our buffalo girls. He came out to see for himself and offer moral support.

Chanel became intoxicated. She was staggering and drooling. The other girls noticed and were quite concerned about her. She fell to the ground and they gathered around with little burps and belches, encouraging her to get up. I jumped on the ATV with a bucket of range cubes to entice the girls away from her. Channel staggered to her feet to go with them.

This distance would have to do. Dr France put a lasso around her horns and tied it around an oak tree. It was shady and quiet. Very efficiently he doctored her eye and released her from the tree.

We had to keep an eye on Chanel for the next hour or so until she was on her feet again. She was not to lay on her side or put her head down on the ground. She did real good. By the next day, she had recovered from her ordeal, but not yet from the "pink eye". The herd was to receive Aureomycin crumbles in their food for the next couple of weeks. This antibiotic would serve both to help Chanel recover and to prevent the illness spreading to the other girls. It worked, No one else came down with the infection. Chanel's eye gradually returned to its beautiful brown color, but with a white spot.

I plotted revenge and destruction for those nasty flies. Hurt and annoy our buffalo girls would they! They would be sorry. We bought more ammunition for the war on flies, though I'll admit that by now it was like closing the corral gate after the buffalo were out. We bought dozens of fly traps. They were unique smelly bottles. The flies would crawl in to smell and couldn't find their way out. They would get caught in the pool of smelly water and drown. And I could watch them. Revenge was sweet.

Sugar had ten beautiful puppies under the porch. They are Golden Retrievers by the way. It didn't take the flies long to find those babies either, or the fleas. The war of the flies raged on. At least I could watch them die in those traps. The fleas didn't give me that satisfaction.

Still the rain did not come. Autumn leaves colored the hills in a beauty that rivaled spring. A few sprinkles fell, but not enough to have any effect on the plants. In November, an exceptionally early snow fell. The snow helped a lot, it soon melted and nourished the parched ground. More importantly for me, it was like dropping an atomic bomb on the flies. They were gone at last.

There will be another war on the flies again next year, I'm sure. But maybe the weather will be on our side next time. Nothing will be left to chance. I'm planning a sneak attack on the flies on the first warm days of spring.

There is a happy ending to Chanel's ordeal. Her eye is now beautifully clear, no trace of her bout with 'pink eye' remains. That makes it all worth while.

Chapter 6   To Auction to Buy Me a Buffalo

A deep metallic clank and boom announced the opening door. Hundreds of eyes riveted to the open space, waiting for the appearance of the next little fellow. An approving murmur greeted his rush into the arena. He backed into a corner, facing the auctioneer in the booth above him. Nearby, a cowboy perched in a protected space. He waved a flapping stick at the cornered calf.

The calf lowered his head and pawed his little front foot, but did not budge. Another cowboy across the arena jumped from his perch to the sandy floor, waving his arms and calling the calf. Running past in a small circle, as if to pick up speed, the little bull thundered across the arena. But the cowboy was gone, safely back on his perch. Confused, but satisfied, the calf turned to face his audience.

Above the auctioneer's head, a lighted sign flashed the weight of this buffalo, 380 pounds. The numbered ear tag showed him to be a seven month old bull calf from the Meistrell herd. The crowd was checking their list to verify his statistics. A voice over the loud speaker reminded them that they were looking at the buffalo who had earned the Best of Show Bull Calf award.

The bidding started high for a bull calf: $1,000.00, $1,100.00, 1200.00, 1300.00, 1350.00, $1400.00. My new friend Janie's card was in the air. 1475.00, 1500.00, 1525.00, 1550.00, 1550.00 again. Do I hear 1550? Are you all through? Do I hear 1550.00? Quiet. Sold for $1525, on his way to Arkansas.

A door opened on the left side of the arena. The little bull looked around at the sound and spotted the opening. In a flash he made his escape and disappeared from view. A satisfied crowd discussed his price and jotted down notes on their auction list, until a loud clanking sound brought their eyes to the arena once more.

That little fellow would not be buffalo burger. Not at that price. Lucky fellow! He would be a herd bull with his own private herd of beautiful buffalo girls to reign over and protect. Mike and Janie had happy smiles on their faces. He was theirs.

Leon and I were at our first Buffalo Auction. We were not buying. In a few weeks, we would be getting 15 heifer calves from the Butterfield Ranch. It was reassuring to see Larry and Kay Butterfield both actively involved in the auction for the Kansas Buffalo Association.

This is a different auction with one of my own babes for sale years later – but it will give you an idea of what I was seeing at my first sale.

We were new to this whole thing and were glad to see our buffalo were coming from a respected ranch. Larry hadn't told us that he was past president of the ABA, among other thing. He had suggested we attend this auction for the education and experience. It was excellent advice.

I was getting a vicarious pleasure watching my new friend Janie bid. It was the next best thing to buying for ourselves – and I didn't have to pay the bill. Janie had already bought the best of show heifer calf from the Wayne Copp herd, as well as this little bull.

I looked around the arena watching the contest between the buyers. The audience was excited and restless. Men, women, and children of all ages crowded together to watch the action. My amazement must have been spoken out loud. "There's no such thing as a typical Buffalo Buff, is there?" Nearby, Arnie laughed in agreement as he too looked around at the crowd. Arnie was not buying either. He had a big herd of his own back in Oregon, he's a lucky fellow too.

Movement caught my attention. Janie's bidding card was in the air again. This was unexpected. A glance down at the sale floor found a large bull calf. He was hitting the scales at 685 pounds and the bidding was slow. Janie won. She called him BB for Bargain Bull – or Burger Bull. I'm not sure which. They would take him home and fatten him up, so he could fatten them up. Something like that anyway.

All too soon, the arena door clanked shut for the last time. The auction was over. Thanks for coming! See you next year. Wild horses couldn't keep me away! But the show was not over by a long shot.

Outside was a long line of pickup trucks and stock trailers of every description imaginable: old and beat up: shinning and new: dirty and clean; borrowed or rented or owned. One by one, they backed up to the load out alley to collect their buffalo. The alleys were covered with black plastic so that the buffalo would not be distracted in their 'run to freedom' which brought them into the trailers.

We were exchanging business cards with new friends and promising to keep in touch. Congratulations were given to our friend Wayne Copp for winning three trophies for his buffalo. We had met him at the American Royal Stock Show in Kansas City two days earlier. He had invited us to his ranch to see his herd and watch the amazing show of getting his buffalo through a squeeze chute for testing and then into a trailer. It had been the most educational and exciting part of our trip to the auction. We had taken a personal pleasure in seeing his animals do so well at the auction. I learned right away that the 'side adventures' we would have would be the most treasured parts of our buffalo trips.

Before next year's auction, we would make a number of visits to Mike and Janie's Horseshoe Mountain Bison Ranch in Greenbriar, Arkansas. I was still getting a great deal of pleasure keeping up with their herd, even though we now had fifteen buffalo girls of our own. A few months between trips made such a difference in the maturity of their buffalo. We see ours every day and the changes are gradual or we don't see them. Plus, the McDaniels had BULLS. They were magnificent.

Of course, we had to visit their herd from the back of a pickup truck. It wasn't safe to be out with their bulls. Oh, and remember BB, the Bargain Bull? He's not only perfectly safe, but spoiled rotten. Mike combs his hair with a brush every day, even down his back. I watched Mike, Janie and their daughter Darla taking turns grooming him for 'their girls'. Mike sits on the side of the pickup truck with a bull's head resting on each knee while he gives them range cubes. Although still young, they seem massive, and gentle, and wild and demanding and dangerous! We've just got to have our bulls soon!

Just when it seemed I couldn't wait a day longer to buy our bulls, it was auction time again. Most auctions are in the fall when the calves are weaned from their mothers. The cows are already pregnant with next year's calves and the expectant moms need a break. The calves are vaccinated and wormed and tested for disease at that time.

We had been looking forward to this fall's auctions for a full year and we were prepared. A fine new stock trailer stood under a just completed shed. The pickup was serviced and ready for action. Our bank account was primed and waiting to be emptied. The big day had arrived.

Our first auction was to be the First Annual Oklahoma Buffalo Association Auction in Perry, Oklahoma, a five hour drive away. We timed our arrival for mid afternoon the day before the auction. Making a bee line for the stockyard, we checked out the animals in the pens and watched as new buffalo were unloaded.

Then it was off to the motel and the 7pm buyers social. Here we could meet the ranchers and learn more about individual herds. Hospitality was outstanding, as was the food and company. This was my kind of party. Everyone was talking BUFFALO!

Morning found us having breakfast with a whole herd of Buffalo Buffs, including our friends Mike and Janie. This was a fine way to start an exciting day. Then it was on to the stockyard for a final inspection and selecting of animals to bid on.

When the doors of the auction house opened, we found the best seats and settled in for action. Bidding began with the females. There weren't many and prices went straight through the roof. Mike and Janie decided not to buy at these prices. They would wait two weeks for the next auction. Our friends from Texas had not come this far to return home empty handed. They bought a beautiful heifer calf and had to pay $2200 for the privilege. We didn't buy yet. Leon and I had bulls on the brain.

Finally the girls had been sold and it was time for the bulls. It was like eating desert first. In came four adorable, perfect little fellows from the Pinkerton herd. I gobbled up the very first one for $1000. Then the audience came awake. His next brother went for $1725. Wow! Then came another pen of four bull calves. I bought the best one for $1000, then another for $900. Janie was looking concerned. What were we going to do with all the bulls? Were we still going to get the larger breeding bulls? Sure! Janie offered to sit on my bidding number for me for safe keeping.

About that time, the cutest little fellow came into the arena. He was small and scrawny, all legs and ears and eyes. There were oohs and aahs all over the room, but no one was bidding. Leon nodded his head 'yes' and my bidder number was in the air for the fourth time. That little guy was ours for $550. I handed my bidder number to Janie with a smile. Fortunately, for me, there weren't many more calves. Mike admitted he had been tempted to take that little guy home if I hadn't.

Next came the yearling bulls. This was more serious. We needed these guys for breeding and I had promised our buffalo girls that I would do a good job of match making. We had chosen three to bid on. They came into the arena together in a group. The best one became ours for $1200 and I marked that a bargain. The third became ours for $1100. Good deal!

There was only one other animal at the auction that I wanted, a truly outstanding two year old. I had talked to his owner and was really excited about this buffalo. Unless the price went out of sight, he would be ours. We got him for $1700 and I considered him a steal. That was it.

We were now the proud owners of seven bulls. We paid our bill and gathered the health papers. Outside was that long line of pickups and trailers. It would be a long drive home. Leon and I conferred briefly and decided to spend the night. The animals could be fed, watered and rested and so could we. Tomorrow would be a fresh day and we could take our bulls home leisurely to meet the buffalo girls.

Eight o'clock the following morning found us at the nearly deserted stockyard. I backed the big stock trailer up to the loading gate like a pro and said a quiet "thanks" to Darla for the instructions on how to back a trailer. The three bigger bulls came running into the trailer first and the center dividing gate of the trailer slammed shut behind them. Soon the four calves appeared and tumbled into the remaining compartment. A slam of the door and they were all loaded. A piece of cake!

Hopping up on the trailer bumper, I matched the numbers in their ears with those on the paperwork. I had discovered how important this simple act could be. A trailer had been loaded the day before with large bulls when one of them simply collapsed from stress and exhaustion. He couldn't get up, so the other animals were off loaded.

That trailer had been backed up to an empty pen. After about an hour the buffalo got up and came out of the trailer. That was when they discovered that he had been loaded into the wrong trailer and was not theirs at all. It was as if that poor buffalo bull was trying to tell them they were making a mistake. Anyway, he taught me a lesson. I'll always check numbers before heading for home with new buffalo.

The trip home was pleasant but uneventful. I kept stopping often to see our bulls and make sure they were all right. Leon wanted to know what I would do if they weren't okay? Who knows! But I'm sure we would have thought of something. Anyway, I just wanted to see them.

Our seven bulls made themselves right at home in the corral. Outside, fifteen beautiful buffalo girls put on their best smiles to welcome these newcomers. For the next ten days, the girls didn't stray from the corral fence for long at a time. When the gates were opened, the girls were there to mingle and show the boys around.

The corral was empty once more and just in time. There were two more auctions coming up. They would be a day and 40 miles apart. We had more than our share of bulls now but would like to have more girls. Off we went to the Sixth Annual Kansas Buffalo Auction.

Once more we headed straight for the stockyards. After a long drive, we needed a buffalo 'fix'. What we found at the stockyard was amazing. There were hundreds of perfect little buffalo calves, both heifers and bulls. All seemed to be as beautiful as the next. Where did they all come from? How could we choose which ones to buy?

A trailer pulled up to off load more buffalo. Jerry Schmidt's trailer was brimming with buffalo. Two eyes were gazing at me from the back end of his trailer, excited but aware of all that was going on. Those eyes were looking all the way into my heart. She was adorable. The tag looked big in her little ear. It had the number twenty four on it. Suddenly the trailer door opened and she was pushed out. She fell on her side to the ground but bounced up like she was made of 'flubber'. She ran like a shot around the corner before any of the others had touched the ground. She was wonderful and I had her number. That little girl was going to be mine!

Leon and I headed to the motel to register and find the 'Buyers Social'. Soon I was showing photos to other buyers of 'our girls'. I was surprised when some of the ranchers wanted to see the 'baby pictures' too. A beautiful evening followed. I wanted to meet everyone there that I didn't know yet and greet friends from last year. There were ranchers, soon to be ranchers, rangers, meat processors, and even a taxidermist. And again, everyone spoke BUFFALO.

Morning found us again at the stockyard. I was running from pen to pen like a crazy person. I wanted them ALL. But with number in hand, I now had to compete with all those others who had come for buffalo.

It was fun to watch the bulls sell, but this time we were waiting for heifers. It wasn't long before number twenty four came in the arena. She was young and small, only four and a half months old. The auctioneer wasn't impressed, but I knew this girl. She was going home with me for only $1,200. I would have paid much more for her.

Leon and I had been so impressed with Lester Lawrence's herd that we bought two of his girls. We didn't want to get carried away, as there was another auction tomorrow. I couldn't pass up a beautiful girl from the Borderline Ranch for only $1150. Prices were slowing as money must have been running out. One of Mike White's girls came in to the arena with an injured eye. She was a fine big girls from a good ranch. I got her for $1025. That was it for today. We'd see what tomorrow brings.

Maxwell, Kansas was the location for the Kansas Department of Wildlife and Parks 11th Annual Buffalo Auction. This was different. It was held out of doors in a cold blowing wind. To view the animals, we climbed up to "walk the planks' of a narrow catwalk. There was a sea of buffalo below us. Wooden bleachers would be the spot for the sale. We decided to get animals from the Garden City herd if possible.

Soon a fine big heifer calf was ours for $1300. Leon spotted a fine buffalo came into the ring and the price was low. Leon's hand was up before he realized it was a BULL. He'll make a fine addition to our herd. A smaller bull came into the arena. He was wonderful. Soon we had a second bull for only $550. Janie looked pained. Did we really know what we were doing?

The next little heifer had Janie excited as well as me. It was a good thing she was buying yearlings. I could have this little black beauty. We settled for these four animals and said our goodbyes.

Heading back to Salina, we picked up the five girls we had bought the day before. We checked their numbers and headed for home. It had been a long day and would be an even longer drive home. My mind was spinning with thoughts of this latest experience, and the beautiful babies in the trailer behind us. We flew through the night without a yawn passing my lips. Now I was dreaming of coming back to the auction with a trailer full of babies to sell. It would bring us full circle. My heart was already full.

The next day, I was watching the new babes we had brought home from Kansas and spotted a yucky mess on one girl's side. Poor babe, I thought, someone must have pooped on her. Then as I watched, the mess grew larger. How was that possible? Oh, NO! It appeared to be COMING OUT OF HER! Soon there was no doubt the mess on her side was her stomach contents and that she had been gored with a horn.

What could we do? The pen was full of animals and it would be unlikely we could separate her from the rest. She at least should have antibiotics to help prevent infection from setting in. We had a dart gun, kind of like a pistol that fired using a CO2 cartridge. I practiced and practiced with it, but each time it fired there seemed to be a different pressure. Maybe the CO2 was being depleted or something. But finally it was time to try darting her and it worked – that time anyway. Another time when we darted, she kicked the dart from her hip – how did she do that?? It was months before we found that feathered dart. It was bent in two and had landed hundreds of yards away. Awesome!

Neighbors came by to see the new babes and scared me with their insistence that if she did not have surgery right away, there was no way the little girl would survive. For advice I called Doc Ken, the top buffalo vet up in North Dakota. He was reassuring, "this is a buffalo not a cow. They are tough, my money would be on her". I almost cried. He went on to say that I should continue to give her antibiotic, but put it in her feed. The darting would be too hard on her.

Delores was in a pen by herself, but the herd did not forget her and not only came by to visit, but comforted her as well

We let the rest of the new babes out of the pen, keeping the gimp we had named Delores, Spanish for pain, by herself so we could medicate her. She seemed to get a little better each day until soon it was time to let her go out with the herd. But she still couldn't keep up. I managed to herd her back into the pen for more treatment and the next time we let her out she kept up fine.

Unfortunately, Delores' story does not have a happy ending. She was with us all that year, but the next winter gave up to pneumonia. We had the vet do a postmortem on her and discovered that she had been gored in the chest as well as the stomach. That had broken ribs which in turn had adhered to her chest wall. It must have pained her every time she breathed, at least in the beginning. And she only had 30% of her lung capacity. Delores was definitely tough and will never be forgotten.

Chapter 7 Solo, Queen for a Day

There's an awful lot of pushing and shoving and nudging with horns when fifteen buffalo girls live together. Seems like when one buffalo gets pushed around, she looks for someone she can 'pass it on to'. In our herd, it was hard to tell at first who was at the top of the pecking order. But from the beginning it was obvious who was at the bottom of that list.

Pool little girl! She was blind in one eye, apparently from an injury or maybe pink eye. All the other girls pushed her away anytime she was within their reach. She couldn't get to the food or the water until everyone else had theirs. All alone, Solo. Trust me, it made your heart ache for her.

Solo was afraid of everything except maybe the dogs. She wasn't able to catch the dogs but they know to stay out of her way. You couldn't much blame her for being afraid. She hadn't known much kindness in this world. Maybe from her mother, but she had been taken from her mother back in December and hadn't found a kind soul since. Now here she was, half blind, afraid and alone, our Solo.

We drive out to the field each day to visit our girls. They would come up to the car for pressed chunks of range cubes. The girls had no fear of the car and were eager for the sweet molasses taste of the cubes. Noses were stuck right into the car in their competition for the treats. But not Solo. She stood on the outskirts of the group and watched with her one good eye.

Buffalo have a good sense of smell and hearing. We began throwing range cubes out to Solo. Of course if there were any other girls around her, they would pick up the cubes and chase her away. To make it easier for her to know a cube would be flying her way, we began calling her name before we threw the treat. Solo would look at us when she heard her name called and would see where the cube landed. She got pretty good at getting them and I was getting better at throwing.

We had two long feed bunks in the corral. They were sturdy ten foot long metal frames with a tough plastic trough. We would put fifty pounds of grain in the feeders usually once a day. This gave us a chance to visit with the girls again and kept them used to coming into the corral. That way, we could round them up just by standing there and calling them to dinner. They knew my voice and would come from any part of the field at my call. Before long, they had grown so much that a third feed bunk had to be added.

You've probably guessed by now, Solo didn't get to eat at those feeders. In fact they chased her right out of the corral. Well, Solo knew her name, so I called her around to the gate where she could eat in peace. Leon made a special little feeder just for her. If another buffalo came around to take her food from her, we pulled the feeder back under the fence using a rope tied to it. After a while, the other buffalo girl would give up and go back into the corral.

While Solo was eating from her special feed pan, we would hold range cubes out to her. It took a few weeks of coaxing, but eventually she took one from my hand. She gradually increased her trust in us and was rewarded with all the cubes she wanted. A few more weeks and she finally permitted a touch.

Most buffalo don't like to be 'petted' and Solo is no exception. But after six month of gentle persuasion Solo does trust us. She no longer hesitates to come up to us for our standard buffalo greeting. I reach out my hand and the girls touch it with their noses. They may not stay or visit in any other way, but rarely will any girl reject this simple greeting.

The days passed into weeks and months, before we knew it summer was gone. The 'girls' had become 'girl ladies'. They were larger and had long horns. Now their skimpy summer hair was giving way to a beautiful winter robe. They weren't babies anymore, they were yearling heifers. Solo was beautiful too. It was a wonderful transformation.

Leon and I had special plans for the fall. It was time to find bulls to add to the herd. I talked to the girls and promised to be a good match maker for them. Leon claimed the right to name the bulls, since I had named the girls. He would call them all George, all of them. If George Foreman could do it so could he.

Off we went to the auction with our brand new stock trailer, pulled by our beautiful, if not so new, pick-up truck. The plan was to find a couple of yearling bulls. You might say we got a little carried away as there were seven Georges in that trailer when it returned home. The two yearlings, four bull calves and one great big wonderful two year old bull. That big guy was immediately dubbed Gorgeous George.

All the Georges were kept in the corral for ten days to get acquainted with their new surroundings. And surrounded they were most of the time. The girls hung around the pen and waited for George's freedom.

Right from the beginning, Gorgeous George was king of the herd. All the girls were crazy about him. He seemed to make each one of them seem special to him. He had eaten range cubes from our hand the third day he was with us. Now his favorite spot was to be parked right in front of the treasure of range cubes, where he could keep an eye on those treats. He made sure half of them would end up in his mouth.

But George did not dine alone. He escorted one of the ladies to dinner each time. You never knew which lady would be with him, but she always proudly stood at his side and happily took her share of his range cubes. Toward the end of that first week, George arrived at breakfast escorting a beaming Solo. What a gentleman! Solo stood at the gate happily gobbling range cubes. George stood at her side licking her hip, more on her than on the food.

Mariah, a spirited buffalo girl used to pushing Solo around, spotted Solo getting the food. She moved in as usual to chase Solo away. Did Mariah have a surprise coming! There was no need for Gorgeous George to defend his lady! Solo turned her head to Mariah with horns blazing and stood her ground. Stunned by this turn of events, Mariah turned tail and left. Gorgeous joined Solo for a bite of food and they happily munched away in unison.

Never had Solo looked so beautiful and happy as she did that day with Gorgeous George. If he never pays attention to her again, I know she will always love him for that glorious time by his side. King George had crowned her "Solo, Queen for a Day".

By all rights that should have ended this chapter. But I wanted you to know that for Solo, it was only a beginning. She has a new maturity about her now. Although her place is still low in the pecking order of the herd, she knows it is her place. She is no longer alone and she is not afraid. Welcome to our herd family, Solo!

Chapter 8 George, George and George

Leon and I filled a bucket with range cubes and set off across the pasture in the Izuzu
Trooper. The herd was grazing at the far side of the pasture. We had released baby
Delores from her hospital ward the day before and we were concerned about her.
Delores was with a couple of yearling girls who were 'nursing' her near the edge of the
herd. She was doing fine.

Delighted at the unexpected visit, the older buffalo girls immediately surrounded our
car. They knew we could be talked out of something special to eat. As usual, their
noses pushed through the open windows with long tongues licking away. Who could
resist a face like that? We were passing out range cubes right and left.

Suddenly a huge figure blotted out the sun and the girls moved out of the way of
mighty Gorgeous George. His face now filled my whole window. "Hello, George", I
laughed. "Come on in. Whoa! Wait George. I didn't mean it! Yipes!" Georges face was
now practically resting on my chest. This was really up close and personal.

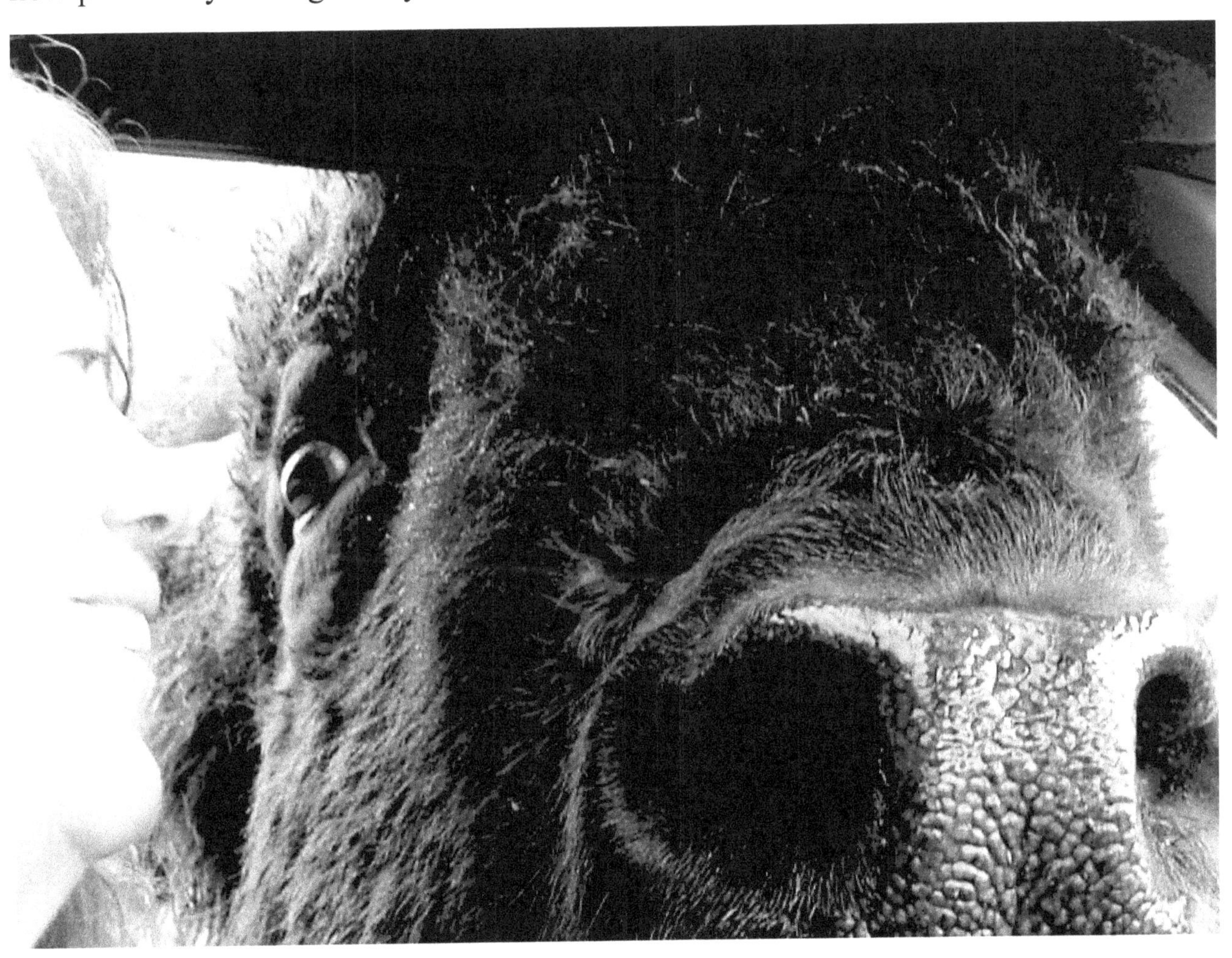

I scrambled for a hand full of range cubes and stuffed them in his big mouth. With his usual dignity, George withdrew his face from my window to chew this mouthful of food. Phew! That was too much. I made sure to fill his mouth as soon as it appeared at my window after that.

Our friend Junior warned us that if George were to get his horns inside the car and get caught, he would tear the side of the car off. As strong as he is, he would probably end up turning the car over with us in it. We know by now that George is gentle clear to the bone. But we also know that he is 100% pure buffalo bull. He would not tolerate being caught with his horns stuck in the car. Junior was right

Quickly the bucket of range cubes was disappearing and I had had about all of the "George in my face" I could handle for one day so I rolled up the window. It was interesting that George immediately understood the glass barrier. He did not have to touch it to know it was solid even though he could see through it. He was offended by my rejection of him, and proudly tossed his head. Looking at Leon's side of the car, George could tell that window was still open for treats. He started around the car.

Passing the front of the car, George suddenly realized he had not properly checked out this white monster that carried us around to obediently. He stopped and rubbed his huge chin across the smooth hood of the car. Harder and wider he pushed, testing its strength and temperament. We were chuckling nervously at his behavior. It was obviously time for us to make our exit. Leon dumped the remaining range cubes out of his window and started the engine. George graciously stepped aside and permitted our departure.

It was now clear that we would no longer be able to visit the herd from the comfort of our Trooper. We would try the pickup for size next time. Maybe the one ton dually would be more of a match for George. This was just one more of the changes taking place now that we had bulls in our little herd.

When it comes to a herd bull for buffalo, most experts recommend a ratio of one bull for every eight to ten cows. We now had twenty two girls and expected to get a few more next year. Three bulls would be the appropriate number for us. Fewer bulls than that could result in 'open' cows who did not have calves. More than three could result in considerable energy being spent on fighting among the bulls. Damage could result and again some of the cows might be missed.

If only one bull calf out of ten is destined to be a herd breeding bull, then the other nine end up on someone's dinner table. Their job is to support the herd that way.

We were in the process of planning the best method of breeding our herd. One plan was to buy three yearling bulls in the fall. The following summer as two year olds, they would breed with the girls. Then a few months later, they would be resold at auction as two year old breeding bulls, hopefully for a profit.

At that time, we would buy three more yearlings for the following year. It sounded like a logical plan. It would prevent inbreeding, make a profit and avoid dealing with older cantankerous bulls. We wanted to go a step further. We would buy bull calves rather than yearlings and keep them for two years. We enjoyed calves and they cost less. By buying extra calves, we could keep the best ones for breeding as yearlings and sell the others in the fall for profit as well.

Once we had Gorgeous George, we were so pleased with him that we took a closer look at a second plan. Other ranchers had recommended we buy quality bulls and keep them as long as they performed and behaved at a peak level. It was a simpler plan, but not without problems. We were looking forward to keeping some of our girls' heifer calves to increase the herd size. But George would be their father and we had to avoid inbreeding. Either the bull or the calves would have to go. That was why we had originally chose to go with plan one. We wanted to keep the calves. Now, what to do!

When all else fails, cheat a little, I guess. We could get more property and start a second herd with George's daughters. The idea was appealing. It would be expensive, but could pay high dividends in the long run. Let's do it! We would keep Gorgeous George.

We still needed two other breeding bulls to help Gorgeous with his ladies. We had eight candidates for the position. I don't know how Mrs. Foreman keeps track of all her Georges. I needed a system. Leon named all the bulls George, but I would give them a middle name too. The two yearling bulls were now called George Jack and George Allen after two of Leon's buddies.

George Jack was a beautiful animal. He looked huge until he got next to Gorgeous, who towered a good foot above him and out weighted him by more than a few hundred pounds. Still, Gorgeous and George Jack really enjoyed wrestling bouts. George Jack wanted to learn to fight and Gorgeous enjoyed having the exercise.

Gorgeous did not bother much with George Allen. He wasn't as athletic and always ducked out of Gorgeous' way, often with a horn butt in the rump. The choice here was simple. George Jack would be given the number two spot. George Allen would go back to auction next year.

Michael George and Red George were calves from the same herd as the yearling bulls. They were miniature versions of their older brothers. Mikey George would stay and Red George would go to auction. There were still four more calves, so Mikey George wasn't yet guaranteed that remaining precious third spot.

There was George Junior who wore ear tag number two. He was from that fine Pinkerton herd and from Custer breeding stock. He was athletic, fearless and curious. A fine little bull to be sure. There was no doubt about his quality, but I was concerned about his temperament.

George Junior was disrespectful to me, his mother. He actually tried to butt me twice through the corral bars in one day. He thought he was entitled to all the range cubes, like Gorgeous, when that big guy wasn't around of course. When I insisted on giving cubes to the other calves as well, Junior butted the bars of the corral. I slapped his little nose and told him to behave. It was the first time that any of the buffalo had threatened me or Leon.

When I gave the other calves cubes again, Junior butted the bars a second time. I smacked him good on the nose this time and told him if he ever wanted cubes in the future, he'd better not do that ever again! He hasn't. Maybe he understood.

Later that afternoon, Junior kissed my cheek through the bars and I had to forgive him. That was a first too. But I haven't forgotten and it worries me. Junior has breeding bull quality, but he may have to do the job somewhere else.

Leon and Amigo Mutt visit with Frankie George

Frankie George and George John are the two bulls from the Maxwell herd. They are fine animals and have personality coming out of their ears. Better known as Frankie and Johnie, they along with sister Delilah are nearly black and are full of curiosity. They are friendly almost to the point of being fearless.

Frankie is much bigger than Johnie. His horns show he must be three or four months older. Johnie and Delilah are almost twins. Delilah has a orange vaccination tag in her ear and Johnie pees out of the bottom rather than the rear. That's about the only way to tell the two of them apart. Leon thinks all three of them look like little devils. They are unbelievably lovable. Johnie enjoys being petted and scratched. Johnie may become the third bull just by winning the "Most Lovable Bull" award.

The last bull calf is Georgito. You know what a little taco is called? Taquito? And a judge is Judgeito. So the smallest George is Georgito. He was the scrawny little guy at the auction who was all legs, ears and eyes. We later learned that he had been born to an older cow, possibly as old as 40. She had very little milk. Georgito was not just young, he was malnourished. Georgito had been with us only a few days when he injured his eye. We came out one morning and found his eye white and blind looking.

Poor Georgito. He had enough problems without this.

We called the vet out to check Georgito. Putting him in the squeeze chute, the doc gave him a shot in the eyelid, antibiotics, vitamins and a dewormer. But when the chute was opened, Georgito collapsed to the floor. Either suffering from fear prostration or from being squeezed too hard, Georgito was unconscious. The vet quickly got into the chute and got his head up, and finally could lift him to his feet. Georgito staggered back into the corral 'nursery' we had set up for him in the wide alley to keep him away from the other bulls. Dr France gave him a fifty/fifty chance of making it though the night.

At first light the next morning, I was at the corral checking on Georgito in my night clothes. He was still with us. All night I had been imagining him cold and still in the morning. Bless your little heart Georgito. Its a strong buffalo heart.

But Georgito was not out of the woods by a long shot. A few days later, he injured his eye again, really badly this time. It was bleeding and appeared to have a cut across the whole width of his eye. This time Dr France sewed Georgito's eyelid shut over his eye. It was not reassuring to learn that this injury and treatment was as painful to him as it would be to me. Poor baby. Again he was given antibiotics – and he stayed on his feet!

A week later, Leon and I put Georgito into the squeeze chute ourselves. Leon removed the stitches from his eyelid. We washed it with a mild salt solution and sprayed it with antibiotic. A spray of purple dye as protection from the sun completed our doctoring. Georgito took it like a soldier – a Buffalo Soldier, fighting all the way. But he was stronger by far than he had been two weeks earlier.

A week later, Leon and I doctored his eye in the same way again as it still had infection. We were mighty pleased with ourselves for being able to take care of Georgito like this. I even gave him an antibiotic injection. We were learning.

Which three Georges would we keep and which six Georges would be sold? Deciding will not be the hard part. Parting with our buffalo children will be the hardest part.

We will have to get used to it. That's what the buffalo business is all about. I tell myself that we are only 'foster parents' to the Georges. They will be ours for only a little while, then we have to let them go. But while they are with us, they will receive all the love, care and nourishing we can give them. They will have a good life here with us. And the Georges will make our lives richer for having them as our 'foster buffalo'.

Georgeito healed and filled out. He looks good.
Beside him is a special feeder for minerals.

Chapter 9 Waiting for Calves

Our pasture is brimming with buffalo now and they are always on the move. As they graze across the pasture, they take a bite of grass then another step. You do not see them move, but soon you notice they have gone quite a way. They eat a LOT of grass, then stop to chew their cud later. Seems that like cows, buffalo have four stomachs or at least four compartments to their stomachs. The first is called the rumen, making them ruminant animals. When the rumen gets full, they rest and regurgitate the food into their mouth to chew at leisure.

OK, it sounds pretty yucky to cough up food to chew it, but the look on their face as they chew their cud is pure contentment. Now think about it..... They have food in their mouth literally all the time. I could handle that. Maybe you could too.

While Leon and I work in an air conditioned and heated shop, when the weather is nice we open the rolling doors at the front and back of the shop to let in light and fresh air. We're working away with the radio playing and become the show for the buffalo. They hang out near the shop to enjoy the music with us. The fence is only about 40 feet in front of the door.

When the shop doors are not open, the buffalo wander on around to another favorite spot to lay down and chew their cud. That spot is out where the road and driveway come together. They stop traffic when they are that close to the road as they are still a novelty in the neighborhood. Its a dirt road without a lot of traffic fortunately, but they do get lots of visitors. We laugh that they are out posing again.

Around mid November, the grass stops growing and soon the buffalo have eaten most of it. Its time for them to enjoy those big round bales of hay. We learned that buffalo's metabolism slows in the winter and they do not eat nearly as much hay as cattle do. The herd size has really grown since bringing home all the new animals from auction this fall and we'll need more hay. This summer, the 15 girls had not been able to keep up with all the grass growth and we had hayed the pasture again. This time we kept all the hay rather than paying for it to be cut by sharing the hay.

We had also gotten this big idea about how to store the hay. We have this wonderful old hundred year old barn next to our house. What if we cut out the back of the big middle part of the barn and store the hay in there out of the weather to keep it in better condition. We could also use it as a "help yourself" feeder where the bison could go in and get something to eat when ever they were hungry. It would save us work and be a lot nicer for them.

This was not to be the last big idea that I had – that failed to work as planned. The buffalo did definitely appreciate their barn restaurant and the hay stored in there gradually disappeared. Winter can be pretty cold and we appreciated not having to go out in it to put hay over the fence to the herd.

Disaster struck early that spring when we found our sweet Ginger dead. What could have caused it?? The herd was fine and even Ginger did not look skinny or anything. We looked around to see any dangers that might have caused her death and saw nothing. Until we looked at the old barn, that is.

When hay is cut and rolled into those large round bales, the bales are held tight with baling twine or a net wrapping. Ours were held with twine. When we put the bales over the fence for the animals it was important to take the twine off first. If twine is caught in the buffalo's mouth as it eats the hay, there is no way to stop it from being consumed. Twine cannot be digested so passes on through the animal. Unfortunately in the intestines it can get tangled and tie off the intestine so that food can no longer pass through. Death soon follows. And the barn self feeder was full of that twine. We're so sorry, Ginger. We love you!

Winter was giving way to Spring and we were getting pretty excited. The girls would be three years old soon and our first calves would be born before long. Buffalo grow slower but live longer than cattle. Although they don't calve until they are three, they will continue to have calves for a longer time than cattle so you will need fewer replacement heifers to keep the herd growing. Its the age old story – everything in life is a trade off. We think this works just fine except that it seems like we've been waiting an awfully long time for the first calves to arrive.

We had joined the Missouri Bison Association as soon as it had formed and headed off for a meeting in North Central Missouri, about a six hour drive. It was wonderful to see the herd at Dan Shepherd's farm and learn from someone who had raised buffalo for years. We left behind 14 year old neighbor Jared to look after the herd. Jared worked in the wood shop after school and in the summer and he had learned all about the buffalo just as we had. When we called Jared to see how things were going, a strained voice told us that one of the buffalo was dead.

Why do things have to happen when we are not there?? By the time we got home the next day the dead buffalo was getting pretty ripe in smell. It was our beautiful Janie.

We had the veterinarian out immediately to try to find out what happened to our Janie. He did a postmortem on her and found her intestines were inflamed. She had not lost weight and looked to be in excellent condition, so he concluded that whatever killed her had happened quickly. We went and checked the herd and found more bad news.

While the herd looked beautiful, many of them had a bloody diarrhea and runny noses. Doc Wooden had no clue what it was caused from and took manure samples back to the lab. Still no clue. Soon Mariah was in serious trouble. She could not keep up with the herd and while she was usually friendly now she would not come to us but rather go the other way.

I went to Dr France to see if he had any ideas. He listened to our sad story and had no clue either. But he started filling hypodermic syringes with medications. There was antibiotics, worm meds, vitamins and who knows what else. I was relived that at least something was going to be done. Then came the shocker. Dr France handed me the box of medication and said "You can give her a shot, can't you?" What? You're not coming? We were on our own.

We did manage to get Mariah into the corral and squeeze chute. Because she was lagging so far behind, it was easy to sort her from the others. And we gave her all those shots. I swear a couple of them looked like they would hold a whole glass of water. We let her loose and prayed she would be OK. Surprise, it made her better. She was in rough shape, but she not only survived, she had her baby a month later and he survived. She did not breed back that summer, so did not have a baby the following year. We counted our prayers answered for Mariah.

But we could not do that to the whole herd and we still did not know what to do about the rest. Dr Wooden suggested that since the problem was in the digestive system that we should give the herd Albon, a med usually used for puppies. It would be gentler on their system than Corid that would usually be used for cattle who had coccidiosis. I was to put it in their water, along with fruit flavored gelatin to make it taste better. That meant locking them in a pen with no access to water that did not have the medicine in it. They were to remain there for three days at least.

Leon was scheduled for hospitalization for prostate surgery at that point and would not be around to help. I filled a big water tank and added the meds, then headed for the hospital to see Leon. The back of my neck was killing me and I thought maybe I had been bitten by a tick there or something. As long as I was at the hospital, I might as well go to the after hours clinic to be checked on myself. The doctor who examined me said he thought it was nerves. I couldn't accept that idea – I'm one of the most laid back people around. But when I thought over the situation, decided he was quite likely right.

Leon did just fine with his surgery and the buffalo were quite co-operative with me. All got better. What a relief! The buffalo liked the water tank and continued to drink from it after they were released from their pen. So I kept it full and the meds in it for awhile. But George discovered he would make the water splash and it apparently felt good on his head. I was watching him play in the water and decided to go to the house to get my camera. I got back just in time to see him turn over the tank. Water weighs eight pounds a gallon and there were hundreds of gallons in that tank. George is a powerful guy.

By now I realized that while buffalo might have up to a thirty year lifespan, that long life was not guaranteed. The herd was better and the calves would start coming any time now. Neighbors brought visitors to see the buffalo and when the herd came up to the pen, Rosie had a long tissue hanging from her behind. I was so excited! We were going to have our first baby! But the neighbor leaned over and quietly said "that is afterbirth. There is a baby somewhere." Rosie would not have left her baby. This was not good news.

Jumping on the ATVs, we went searching for the still born calf and found it. Oh no...... The day before I had been out with the herd in the Trooper and had fallen asleep in the pleasant sunny day. I was vaguely aware of Rosie walking around the car talking to me. She had known something was wrong.

I went to check on Rosie to see how she was holding up and saw a foot hanging out her butt. What? We found the baby, how could there be a foot? I headed for the house to call the veterinarian but halfway there I had second thoughts. Could I really have seen what I thought? I went back and sure enough there was a single foot quite visible. OK, get the veterinarian out here!

Doc Wooden wanted us to get her in the squeeze chute and he was heading our way. Rosie was close by, but she was not feeling very good. I tried everything I could to get her to come in the pen, even pulling on her horns. It went against everything I knew about buffalo to be out there pulling on her, but I was desperate. I cringe looking back at what I did that day. But we got her where she needed to be and the doc arrived. Seems that Rosie had twins – rare in bison. And the second baby was breech, turned around backwards with only one foot where it could come out. She could not deliver that babe on her own, but now she had help.

Rosie was fine and I had a fresh baby, still born, right there. I decided to take that babe to Springdale, Arkansas, a 40 minute drive away. They have a state lab there that can run tests to find out what is wrong. In view of the lack of diagnosis on whatever had killed Janie, I thought they could run some tests to see if there was any disease present. Their results come back as "uterine insufficiency", Rosie was simply not mature enough to carry twins to full term. They could tell me all the diseases that they tested for and all were negative. We still had no clue. Nothing like that has ever surfaced again in our herd so we'll never know. Just count our blessings that the rest of the herd survived.

Chapter 10   The Babes Are Here At Last

Rosie is my favorite girl, so you can imagine how happy I was that she survived her ordeal. Buffalo have a pecking order as to who is most dominant, and Rosie is not near the top, just somewhere in the middle. But if I go out to the pasture and call the 'girls', Rosie always heads for me. The others know that she leads them to food and they follow her. Thank you Rosie! If Rosie's twins had survived, we would have had more than 100% calf crop that year in spite of the illness. Every other girl had a baby between May 15th and May 30th.

Dulce Ann was the youngest when she came to us, but hers was the first babe we laid eyes on. She was so tiny and adorable.

We were so busy falling in love with little Sweet Pea that we were surprised when Jared said "Look out there!" Eve was way out in the field nursing a baby. Which came first? We don't know – and it does not matter. They are beautiful healthy babies.

The camera was soon my constant companion as my mission became to capture pictures of every precious babe and their mothers. I would shoot a couple rolls of film and head to town to get them developed so I could see what the pictures looked like, double prints too. Soon I had a photo album in progress plus a whole box of pictures that did not make it into the album. Children who came to see the buffalo were allowed to rummage through the box for pictures as souvenirs.

Before long, there were hundreds of pictures and I cannot share them all with you, just some of my favorites. Within two weeks there were twelve of these darlings running around the pasture. It had been a long wait but they were here at last! My camera was BUSY.

It was so exciting to go out in the field every day and see who was going to have the next babe and if we were lucky, we would be there in time to see the baby born, get up the first time and suckle for milk. That first mothers milk was critical for a new born bison calf. It supplied colostrum which gave the babe immunity from disease until its own immune system kicks in a few months later. Once the babe had found its mother's udder, we knew it would be just fine. Here are some of the steps in giving birth that we caught with Jacqueline.

The baby dives into the world feet first with its head between the legs. When we see the nose like this, we are just minutes away from birth. Once the head comes out, the baby literally squirts into the world.

Jackie wasted no time resting, but got immediately to her feet and started cleaning the new born babe. He looked like he was interested in his new world.

I am constantly amazed to see a new born babe try to get up the first time and walk on unsteady legs within minutes of birth. Nature does not give him a rest to get his wits about him. The urge to get to his feet and find his mother's milk is primal within him. Within the hour he will be learning to hop, run, and will start exploring the world around him.

How could you not fall in love with a little face like that?

I was sitting on the ATV using the zoom on the camera and Amigo Mutt, the golden retriever, was hanging out with me. Jackie thought he was getting too close and came after him. The babe's feet were out but not the head yet. She was in heavy labor, but boy she was still able to protect herself and her babe.

What really surprised me was that when she was satisfied that the dog was gone, she returned to the exact same spot where she had been before. I felt blessed that Jackie and the other mothers trusted me enough to let me stay near them like this.

It was Friday's turn to have her baby and I was not there in time to see the birth. When I came out to check on the herd, Friday was so proud of her babe that she brought it right up to the ATV for me to see. Oh, Dear. This little guy was TINY – maybe 20 pounds. He must have been premature and he was so cute! I named him Rusty as he was a deeper red than the other babes.

Before long I became concerned that Rusty was not nursing. He needed that colostrum to provide immunity. When it became clear that he was not getting that milk, we devised a plan to give him a bottle of lamb's milk replacer with beef colostrum in it. Leon would drive the Trooper into the field with 14 year old Jared in the back seat. I would try to lure Friday away from the babe with food. Jared was to jump out, grab the babe and put him in the car.

Well, that did not happen. There was no way Friday would leave that babe. She was off away from the herd and was keeping her babe at her side. It was on to plan two. Because Friday trusted me so much to bring the babe to me, I would try to give the bottle to Rusty with Friday right there. I don't get off the bike ever, but felt confident in this plan. I was poking the nipple at the little guy's nose when he became shy and ran under Friday – BUT he grabbed her udder that was hanging there. He didn't drink, but he definitely had put it in his mouth. Within the hour Rusty was nursing.

You have to understand that we were really new to all this and did not always exercise good judgment when dealing with herd problems. Fortunately there has been no incident that we regretted and we have learned to exercise proper caution around the herd. Its kind of sad, but we have to think of people before buffalo and may not be able to successfully fix every problem that arises for the sake of our own safety and that of others.

It was Rachael's turn to have her calf and we were there in time to witness the miracle of birth, then watch that baby find its mother's milk. We were so glad that we had buffalo in our yard! It was a blessing.

A few hours later, I took a spin around the pasture to see how the herd was doing.

Rachael and Gorgeous George were together in the woods at the corner of the pasture. There was no baby with them. What? Now where could that little one be. Bison don't park their babes in the grass the way deer do and Rachael was grunting out a call for her babe with no answer. I drove around on the ATV for awhile with no luck finding the babe. It was time for reinforcements. I got Leon to join me in the search on the other ATV. See how we had progressed? The four-wheelers were invaluable to us now and we had 'his' and 'hers'. Together we searched until darkness was complete but were no closer to finding that babe. Maybe it had got under the fence and could not get back and was lost in the neighbor's field. We'll look for her in the morning.

Morning came and still Rachael was without her beautiful calf. I came back to the house to fix breakfast before resuming the search. The dogs started barking in the yard and I glanced out the window to see what was going on. There was the babe laying under the gate to the pasture right next to the house! What a relief to have found her! Leon and I went rushing out to get her but when we were about ten feet away she jumped up and ran into the pasture, then back out through the barb wire strands of fence like it was not there. She disappeared around the corner of the hundred year old barn.

We were stunned on so many levels. We had not expected her to be so fast or to go through the fence, or to run away like she did. But most of all we were amazed to see her injuries. Her tail had been chewed off and there were injuries to her butt and leg. The dogs were not attacking her – they knew better by now. Maybe coyotes or someone else's dog had gone after the babe.

We didn't have time to figure that out now, we had to find and retrieve our lost babe and we ran for the ATVs. We couldn't spot that babe anywhere and Leon headed up the road to see if she went that way. I noticed one of the front doors of the barn was open and went to check that out.

OH, Look what I found! Hiding with her nose stuck in the corner was the babe. She seemed to think if she could not see me, I could not see her. Well, it must have worked the day before.... I closed the barn door. When Leon returned from his search, we slowly entered the barn and closed the door behind us. We threw a quilt over the babe and carried her out to the Trooper then headed for the herd.

In the back of the car, when the babe peed out her back end rather than the bottom we knew we had a little girl. Pulling up in front of the herd, we opened the back of the Trooper to let her out. George came over to investigate the open door and was rewarded by a kick in the nose from a very frightened babe. That didn't work. We pulled up further ahead of the herd and I lifted the babe to the ground. This time Rachael saw her babe and came rushing to her. She followed the little thing around, licking her wounds and grunting. It was nearly an hour before Little Wonder had another meal of mother's milk.

Wonder's wounds healed just fine but her tail did not grow back. I read that in Canadian parks, an estimated one in ten bison calves loses its tail to predators. What makes that so impressive is that it means that many escaped their attackers. Little wonder adjusted and stayed a member of the herd.

On the National Geographic website is a video of a bison babe who was swept away by the river and attacked by a wolf but survived. It is amazing to watch. If its still online, you can watch it at https://www.youtube.com/watch?v=K6TnWW1s4hE Isn't it wonderful to be able to share online?

Wonder's tail never grew back, but she healed just fine

We knew we had a problem – there were too many buffalo in our pasture. Now add another twelve babies and WOW, something had to be done. Since we had decided to keep Gorgeous George, we did not need all those other bulls. That was certainly a place to start. But if we wanted to keep most of our calves we would need more pasture. The hunt was on seriously now for property to expand our farm.

Our buddy Junior was always bragging about his beautiful 40 acres and he was not doing much with it. The aerial chart from the county showed it was a beautiful property: square, fenced, nice barn, big pond and small pond. What was not to like? Would you sell it Junior? Sure, was the reply. Would you give me $40,000? That seemed quite reasonable. Junior wanted to think it over. The next day he came back with Would you give me $50,000? A little more hesitant this time, OK. Let me think about it he says. The next day it was Would you give me $60,000? Yes, Junior, but that is it. Let me think about it he says.

Junior approached another neighbor and asked for $70,000 but the answer was negative. Guess you can't fault a guy for asking. We bought it from Junior for $60,000 and went to work getting it ready for the bison.

Meanwhile, word was out that we had a couple of breeding bulls for sale and soon had buyers come to the farm. We agreed on a price for the animals and that we would semen test the bulls to make sure they would be good breeders.

Doc Wooden came out to do the semen test on the two bulls. Those bulls were not happy with the situation. The first bigger bull to go into the squeeze chute messed up the equipment so that it was not usable. The rear door no longer closed. Maybe it was fine for calves but not for bigger animals. There would be no semen testing so we released the bulls from the pen and called the buyers to apologize. To our surprise, both buyers said the expect they will take them anyway. OK. That meant we had to catch those bulls again in the pen.

It was surprisingly easy to catch those guys again. They had not minded the captivity at all and wanted to be treated 'special' again to get treats without sharing with George and his ladies. Now there were two less mouths to feed.

We were no longer feeding any grain to the herd. There was no way to put out the food without the herd 'helping' and it was just too dangerous. Besides there were way too many animals to feed and they really did not need grain. But we did want to give the babes some special treatment and bought a Creep Feeder. This was a metal box with a fence around it and openings that only the babies could get through. We filled that box with grain and let the babes come in to help themselves.

At the feed store a lady was telling me a story about her creep feeder. Seems too many calves had gotten in at one time and were jammed in so tight that they could not turn around to get out. Fortunately they discovered the problem before any babes were lost and they had to take the feeder apart to get the calves out. The salesman at the feed store said they sold extensions to make the pen larger to prevent such a thing from happening. So we added the extensions to the fence.

Yes they really can get through the bars
even with that sideways bar across the entrance

Leon was out on the tractor and spotted a calf in trouble in the creep pen. The little bull had tried to go through the side of the fence where the extensions were added and now he was stuck tight. He had already collapsed from exhaustion trying to get out. We had to lead the herd far away then cut the metal bars to get that babe out.

We had already had one incident where a cow had jumped into the creep pen and drug it around the pasture until the fence came apart to release her. It seemed that though this was a quality piece of equipment, it just did not hold up to buffalo. We moved the feeder into the corral and bought a creep gate to add to the corral. Now the calves had all the room they could possibly need. The gate itself would still close over the creep entrance and we could lock the calves in once they were inside. Now that would really come in handy!

This turned out to be the way we would sort the babes from their mothers to wean them. We stopped putting feed in the bin, and started putting a little at a time in a feed bunk. The babes wanted that so much, they would come in the pen even when I was still there. I would sit on the end of the feeder and watch the show. The bigger calves would claim the spots further away from me. Little guys would get pushed closer and closer to me. But they were smart. It didn't take them long to learn that I would not harm them and they could get all the food they wanted if they stayed near me. It was fun. When it was time to catch them, I would wait until all had come inside then just get up and close the gate. They were caught.

Chapter 11   Summer at the Buffalo Farm

Gorgeous George is at his finest in the summer time and thats a real good thing because his is the most important job in the herd, making buffalo babies. Now, Guys, you might think that is a really good job – and George would undoubtedly agree with you. But its not that simple.

The bull first has to determine which cow is ready to be bred by checking her hormone level in her urine, EVERY cow's urine, every day. Whenever he sees or hears a cow pee, he heads her way to check it out. If he missed it streaming out, then he smells the ground where it landed. He sniffs the smell way back into his sinus for testing. If it reads positive its time to go to work. Otherwise, its back to what ever he was doing.

Once George finds a ripe girl he has to seriously court her. The cows get to choose which bull breeds her, so if he is not really, really nice to her then she would not give in to his courtship. And she is not easy. He has to court her for at least a day. Sometimes while he is doing that, he doesn't have time to check the rest of the ladies.

So while George is busy, the other bulls in the herd happily step in to help. Of course those ladies know this is the second string team and want to hold out for that handsome big guy that hasn't noticed them yet. But the bulls are persistent and the girls are beginning to want to be bred. Once a cow has given in, George can't waste any more time on her and chases the younger bulls away from the next cow. This goes on and on all summer. It is called the RUT. You are probably familiar with deer rutting in the fall in order to have babies in the spring. Buffalo rut in summer with a nine month gestation or pregnancy and babies are typically born April through June.

The oldest girls all had babies this summer and they have to provide milk for the little ones. Buffalo are not fully mature until they are seven even though they breed for the first time in their second summer and have their first calf on roughly their third birthday. These young mothers are still growing themselves in addition to nursing their young. Now they are expected to get pregnant with a calf for next spring. Grass is at its prime in the spring, providing the best nutrition during this important time of calving and nursing so they will be in good condition to go into the rut.

Josie and Little Joe

The buffalo calves were pretty small at birth, somewhere around fifty pounds. This is nature's way of preventing problem births. Beef cattle have been selected by ranchers for bigger and bigger animals and as result often need help from farmers to pull the big calves out at birth. Buffalo don't want help and since they have not been bred by man for centuries are designed by nature to not need any help by being smaller at birth.

You saw that a newborn buffalo is on his feet, running, playing and exploring the day he is born. Its a miraculous thing to watch. You can watch videos of it on my facebook page at https://www.facebook.com/carol.klein.988. If all that is not enough, he makes friends with other calves right away, bonds with his mother, and gets acquainted with the other members of the herd. He is also incredibly curious, tasting and smelling anything he comes across. When he tastes something good that agrees with him, he will eat it every time he comes across it in his wanderings. He also watches the others eating and learns from them. I guess its what you would call a 'crash course' in buffalo school. The babes are having a wonderful time and its a joy to watch.

All buffalo have horns, both male and female. Some bison ranchers choose to remove, cut off, the buffalo's horns. Maybe it gives some cushion of safety for a person responsible for them, but not a lot. From what I have seen, they are more likely to butt or throw an offender than to gore him. I find that interesting as it indicates they want the problem to just go away rather than trying to 'kill' the offender. They are still really dangerous, horns or not! And they look goofy without their horns as their hair hangs all over.

You can pretty easily tell the age and sex of a buffalo by looking at their horns. The more curve to the horn, the older the animal. A bull's horns are much bigger around – and his head is much bigger than a buffalo cow. Sometimes a horn gets broken off and it never grows back. Or maybe just the tip gets broken off when they are babes. I find that the horns are the first step in identifying the particular animal you are looking at. Of course if the animals is exceptionally big you can be reasonably sure that it is a bull. And a younger bull, while not big has a wider head and bigger horns than a female his size. His horns also tend to stick straight out in a 'spike' while young females horn tend to start curving sooner.

While buffalo babies are a pumpkin color when they are born, by the end of summer they will have grown out the brown color of the buffalo herd. The brown starts to show first in a streak across the back where a horse would have a mane. They also start to get brown around the face. They are pretty cute when they have that variegated mix of colors and it shows they are growing up.

Those little guys still look like babies until they turn brown, but they really are growing fast. Between the richness of their mother's milk and all the forage they have learned to eat, they will add another three hundred pounds to their original fifty in their first six months of life. You can feed them extra grains, but they don't need it. They may get big faster, but no healthier. And they will not end up any bigger in the long run, just fatter. I see the fat as masking their true genetics. I prefer to eat grass fed bison rather than giving them grain, as I get enough fat and don't need to add any. In bison, the muscle, ie meat, does not marble with fat. Instead fat is deposited in given areas, especially between the skin and muscle where it acts as insulation against heat and cold. That summer sun is not bothering them in the slightest.

For the farmer who cares for the bison, his job is pretty much to take care of the land and fences rather than the animal. They are pretty capable of taking care of themselves. We need to have salt blocks out for them and a mineral feeder is a good idea as 'health insurance' for the herd. Unless the field is over stocked with animals there is no need to put out hay or grain. At this point, we are rapidly reaching the over stocked stage. Its a good thing that Junior sold us that new 40 acres and we'll be working hard on getting that ready for many of these animals with us now.

We're still fighting flies. We tried predator wasps, but I could not tell that it was helping. Its pretty much fly traps, rubs and good nutrition to try to keep them under control. I don't think there is ever a summer without some pink eye here at our farm though some years are worse than others. Did I tell you we called the farm Oakcreek Buffalo Ranch? Our woodworking business was on Oakcreek Drive in California, and was called Oakcreek Woodworks. We just used the same name in the farm as the business.

This mower was too small and was replaced by one ten foot wide

Leon likes driving his tractor and that is a good thing too. Its important to mow the grass and weeds in the pasture. It keeps competition down when the weeds are mowed. With the grass, if we cut off the seed heads it has a couple of benefits. One is that the tall seed heads can irritate the eyes of the grazing animals and contribute to the spread of pinkeye. The other is that by cutting off the seed heads, the grass keeps on growing just like your lawn does. If the grass is allowed to produce seeds, it thinks its job is done for the season and stops growing. We call the mowing results keeping the grass in a vegetative state.

Here in the Ozarks, Fescue has become the dominant grass. It has a toxin in its seed stalk that leads to the seed head. This toxin affects the ability of cattle to control their body temperature. I have not seen the buffalo have this problem. Cattle stand in ponds to try to cool off. For buffalo, the water is a play area for socializing and may help keep the flies from annoying them. They use their tails to throw water over themselves and I'm sure causes the flies to get off each time. Fescue is what is called a cool season grass. It goes dormant in the heat of summer, but grows really well in spring and fall. Clover is the same way, and we have lots of white clover plus some very small yellow clover and large red clover.

In mid summer, the Bermuda grass is in its prime but our buffalo don't really care for it and will not graze it if there are other grasses. And there are many kinds of grasses in the pasture. I can sit on the ATV and count as many as eight kinds of grasses surrounding me. One pretty common one for example is Foxtail. I bet you can guess what that one looks like. Around Thanksgiving the temperatures fall and day length gets short so that even the cool season grasses stops growing. Soon it would be time to start putting out hay for the herd. They will spend the winter doing what I call 'recreational grazing'. They may not be getting much to actually eat, but they will get some and they like to graze, its their nature.

Some weeds are edible too for the buffalo. They eat some rag weed for example. When the plants are small, its sometimes easier for them to eat the weed than to eat around it. And it has plenty of protein and nutrients in it. But plants have a protective mechanism, usually bitter taste for example. Its usually eaten in moderation with other plants. During drought years when forage is poor, the buffalo would often eat ragweed and the prickly thistle flowers rather than depend solely on hay. At least it is grazing and the weeds are fresh.

This summer we were concentrating on getting Junior's 40 acres ready for buffalo. It was fenced all round, but we beefed up the fence with taller posts and a couple extra strands of wire along the lowest side. Then we hired a professional fence guy to come in with electric. We were not experienced with electric fence and it had a definite learning curve. When brush and brambles grew up in it, it could short out and it would be really hard to work on. But we added one hot strand on top and one near the bottom out in front of the existing fence. We also decided to divide the property into two pastures, each with a pond.

At the NBA summer conference trade show, we compared the types of squeeze chutes made specifically for bison. We managed to score delivery of a High Hog model that was used as a show model. The local Sibley manufacturing company who helped us with the first pen designed a much more sophisticated pen and sweep leading to the High Hog. We also built a large holding pen near the wonderful old barn. Water would have to be hauled in and kept in a big rubber tank when animals were confined. We felt like we were ready to move many of the animals from the house over to the new property.

All the extra bulls would be sold this fall. We had already sold two and now had a buyer for Frankie George and Johnnie George. There were still the extra calves, now yearlings, that we bought last year plus the six bull calves born this year that would go to auction in November.

In addition to the bulls we were intending to sell, we also moved some of the girls we bought at auction last year and the heifer calves born this year. It made a nice little herd, but would be reduced by the auction soon and would have room to hold more of next years calves as well.

Our home sits right in the middle of the original buffalo herd's pasture. The 40 acre square has a kind of horseshoe area from the road to the house. At the road sits the original farm house built around 1909. We had to remodel that house to keep it habitable and it is a real asset to the farm. Also in that area is a large yard where big round bales of hay can be stored, a hundred years old barn, the shop where we work, a big building where we store wood, equipment and stuff like that. Later we added a barn for hay.

The really nice thing about this arrangement of the farm is that the buffalo almost totally surround us. Sometimes they have been in the yard as well, but that is another story.... I can usually look out a window and spot the buffalo. Me, I'd rather be out there WITH the buffalo. But like most folks, we need to earn our living. We're really fortunate to work at home so that we don't waste hours a day commuting back and forth. UPS comes every day to pick up boxes packed with the product we made that day.

A century ago, most folks lived on farms. That is just not the case any longer. Those of us fortunate enough to live in a more rural area can actually choose to farm as well as work in town. Those farms are typically small but they do give the life style that many of us crave. It supplements our incomes a bit as well and allows us to have and do other things we desire. Mostly I think we just enjoy having our own space around us and being close to nature.

When work is done for the day – and I do enjoy my work – my real quality time begins when I head for the pasture to join the herd. Sometimes I am in the Trooper but more often than not I am riding on the ATV. The buffalo herd is different now that the bulls are here. When I ride out in the ATV the first thing I look for is Gorgeous George. I don't want to get too close to him. He is getting really big now and I have to consider him dangerous. When I identify him in the pasture you can rest assured that he is looking right at me. He is aware of all that is going on in the pasture and its his job to ensure the safety of his herd.

I make eye contact with George from a distance and nod my head at him in acknowledgment that I'm in his world and he is in charge. Only when his authority is recognized does he turn his head from me to graze or see to his ladies.

George only chased me one time and I deserved it. I had a seeder on back of the ATV this spring scattering clover seeds to improve grazing in the pasture. Clover is a legume that fixes nitrogen in the soil to act as fertilizer for the grasses and it also provides a sweet, very nutritious forage for the herd. But I had finished seeding everywhere except where the herd was laying to chew their cud. As I came close with my flying seeds to try to get that last area, George let me know in no uncertain terms that I was not welcome. He didn't chase me very far and I don't think he intended to hurt me. But definitely he let me know my behavior was not 'proper' around his herd.

I may be staying at a distance from George, but not from his ladies. Those girls were my buffalo children and you know how it is with mothers. Children may grow up, but they are always children to their mothers. I love to watch and listen to the sound of them grazing. If they come close to the ATV, I hold out my hand to them and they touch it with their nose. Its a simple greeting but is very welcoming for me. They may stay to rub on the ATV a little – they like to rub on things – or they may just go back to grazing.

You can't imagine how pleasant and relaxing this environment is for me. Maybe I was a buffalo in another life or something. It certainly is good life for them, eating, socializing, playing and having babies with no other jobs or worries. They are really lucky to be on top of the food chain. They don't have to worry about danger from anything except people. And I certainly hope they don't start worrying about me. Those first 15 girls at least are completely safe from me, yet I know somewhere along the line buffalo will be eaten. And those who are eaten will be some of my grandchildren playing around me. My job will be to see that those lead a very good life while they are with me.

I had a new female dog named Lady who liked to ride the ATV with me, sitting on the gas tank right in front of me. The problem was that I could not get too close to the herd when she was riding with me and if I stopped, she would want to get off and run around which could upset the herd. I kept her on a leash with the other end around my wrist. This particular afternoon the herd was just laying around chewing their cud, so Lady Dog and I went for a ride around the pasture.

As we crossed the curving dam of the pond, the left rear tire ran over the leash that was dangling from my wrist and was pulling my hand down under the wheel. I grabbed hold with the other hand to keep from getting pulled off. Unfortunately that was where the gas lever was and the bike lurched forward. Suddenly my feet were flying over my head backwards. It was like Kung Fu or something, just flipped me off the bike and on to the bank of the pond laying on my back.

I could not get up. Something was wrong with my left leg. The bike was still going but it was about 30 feet away. I'd never make it there. It was a pleasant June evening and we had already finished dinner. It would not be completely dark until around nine o'clock. Leon would not miss me. He was used to me being out for hours with the herd. He had the air condition on and was watching TV. He would never hear me if I called for help. But the buffalo would hear me and would think I was calling them for treats. Better to be quiet.

I was beginning to tire and it was getting dark. Lady Dog had finally realized that I was in trouble and was sticking by my side. If the buffalo had come then it would have doubled the danger I was in. I needed to call for help. Neighbors down the road had come to sit outside in the pleasant evening and heard my calls for help. I saw headlights coming across his pasture and raised up thinking someone was getting close enough to hear me. He saw the bike before he saw me. Soon Ted was standing at the fence to find out the problem and went for help.

The women stayed to direct the ambulance while Ted got Leon and told him the situation. The ambulance came down to the pond to get me with plenty of folks in vehicles and bikes as well. My feet had been in the warn pond water which was fine. Now, though, they were talking about the leaches on my feet and legs. What? YucK! NOOOOO! I was ready to check out at that point. Leon broke his glasses when he slipped on the wet edge of the pond trying to get down to me. Then it was off on an ambulance ride with lights flashing, the first time ever for me. Of course the buffalo wanted to come to but getting everyone out of the pasture while keeping buffalo in was not my problem.

My hip had been dislocated and had to be set. There had been more leaches on my legs when they cut my pants legs off. I was past caring, or maybe it was the meds they had given me. Leon said I was screaming bloody murder when they put the hip back in joint, but the doctors told him I would not remember and I don't. The next day was my birthday, June 14, and I was in the hospital to celebrate. I can't complain too much though as I ended up with four birthday cakes that year. I was lucky. The doctor told me that seventy percent of the time the hip broke with that injury. Mine did not break. For the next six weeks I was on crutches to get around and trust me, that was no fun. The worst part was no ATV for me during that time to visit the buffalo.

Most visitors to the farm think all the buffalo look alike, they all are brown and have horns. But on close inspection with an artist's eye they are each very unique in appearance. They are unique in personality as well. They also have good days and bad days just like you and I. This uniqueness of the animals is another of one of my pleasures in knowing them. As more and more animals come into the herd it will become harder to know each one as well as I do these.

Actually, buffalo personalities are quite pleasant. However, they do have a pecking order and challenge each other continually to maintain or improve their status in the herd. This insures that the strongest, most fit animals will get the best food and the opportunity to reproduce. The time this dominance becomes most noticeable is when food is put out in the feed bunks. There will be shoving, running from one feeder to another, the point of a horn to anyone who does not get out of the way in time from an animal more dominant than them.

Grass is the great equalizer for the herd. It is available to all. The dominant one will lead with the others fanning out in her wake, always on the move, eat and step, eat and step. If they are startled or danger threatened, they move as a group to get away amazingly fast. Typically though they will stop without going very far, to see what it was that startled them AND to fight back if they think they can handle that. Even though their pecking order caused them to fight among themselves, they band together against danger. Some do their part by keeping away and being in charge of the younger members of the herd. Others have a personality that sends them after the danger to protect the herd. Together they make the family we call the herd. I call them 'my girls' but I do claim the boys as my own as well.

I do have a problem with one of my girls. She seems to be determined to find out if she is more dominant them me. I had bought Lolita and Leona at auction from Lester Laurence's herd at the Kansas sale. Both are fine girls and George had undoubtedly bred them this summer for calves next spring. You could see mounting marks on their hips where he had held them for mating. I had to treat Lolita like George and keep my distance from her. I had tried bullying her back, but she would come around to the side of the ATV where I was more vulnerable so that didn't work. Keeping away from her was not working real well either. She was relentless in trying to catch up with me when ever I moved away.

Lolita tried to get me when I was in the Izuzu Trooper as well and it was rapidly being covered with dents. Of course some of those dents came from George as well as he liked to 'play' with the car. One day he stuck his horn into the spare tire on the back. When it exploded, it was the only time I saw George get startled enough to jump back. My 13 year old niece was visiting this summer and I taught her to drive the stick shift in the Trooper. Her favorite thing was to drive by Lolita and let her bang into the car.

Accidentally I finally discovered how to 'protect myself" from Lolita when I was visiting the herd. I would drive over to some of the original 15 girls and they would chase her away from me. I thought that over and realized they were not protecting me, rather were disciplining her because her behavior was not acceptable to them. The girls didn't like Lolita but George thought she was wonderful. Men..... And I worried – keeping a dangerous animal in the herd was asking for trouble.

I messed up one evening when I came in from visiting the herd and left the gate open. Whoops! At six o'clock the next morning, Neighbor Ted was knocking on our door, telling us that the buffalo were 'over on him', meaning his property. What we found was that George and all his ladies who had not calved yet had gone roaming. But the new mothers had all stayed behind. As a result, George and his ladies were hanging out on the other side of the fence from the mothers.

Leon and I put range cubes in feed bunks, and tied one behind the Trooper and the other behind the bike. We drug them to the wanderings herd and let them start eating. Then we began pulling the feeders home. Anytime the herd stopped, we stopped and waited for them to start eating again. Soon we had led them all home except George. He was not happy at what we had done, but had no choice but to join his ladies. As he passed the Trooper, he shook his big head at me and his horn shattered the driver's side window of the car. He was kind of astounded by the results and pretty proud of himself. I thought we got away pretty lucky to get them all back home with that as the only damage.

Chapter 12   The New Farm in Fall

The days gradually became shorter and the heat of summer was giving way to fall. The dusty buffalo were beginning to glow with a velvet-like cover of wool. They were starting to grow their winter coats and looked really good. Fall rains made the cool season grasses come out of dormancy and grow again to help the buffalo put on weight in preparation for winter. We sorted off the calves in the creep pen and moved them by trailer out to the new farm twenty minutes away. It was a little harder, but we also managed to capture some of the other younger animals we felt should go back to auction to reduce herd size.

Moving many of the buffalo out of the pasture and the grass growing beautifully created a much better environment for the herd that fall. At the new farm, the pasture had not been grazed all summer and the grazing there would be a smorgasbord for the ones who moved. They were so busy exploring and enjoying their new home that they quickly settled in. We had been creep feeding the twelve calves born that spring and planned to keep the girls to begin to grow the new herd.

Being eager to learn and experience farming a buffalo herd, we also decided to sell one of the heifer calves. Dulce's Sweet Pea won that lottery. She was not necessarily the prettiest, but she was a good eater and the oldest girl. She was the biggest. had put on weight fast and would show well at the sale.

The cross fence that divided the farm into two pasture was three strands of electric that I could actually step over. So could the buffalo as it turns out. I would come out to check on the herd and they would come running, jumping over that cross fence in the process. They knew range cubes would be coming for their eating pleasure. It was inevitable that feet would twang against that wire of the fence. The result was that the post holding the fence in the lower areas were pulled from the ground. If the wire touches the ground it would 'ground out' the fence so that it was no longer 'hot' to the touch. Not only that, the wires would go flying and some even caught in the trees. So much for cross fencing into two pastures that way.

There was a serious learning curve when adding electric fencing to the pasture. It seemed to always be shorting out somewhere and brambles had quickly grown up to hide problems if not create them. Squirrels chewed the rubber coating off wires that carried electricity around the corners. They likely got quite a charge out of that, but the damage was done and we had quite a puzzling time trying to locate where that short had occurred.

One day I was visiting the herd and found that the electric fence was not fully charged. I was walking the fence line trying to discover where the short was. When I was ready to head back to the car in the center near the barn, the herd was all the way on the other side of the property as far away as they could be. It was a beautiful day and the return was down hill, so I started to jog down across the pasture. Before long I heard running behind me and looked back to find the whole herd running along after me. How did they get there? You wouldn't think they could possibly run that fast but here they were.

I would look over one shoulder and the buffalo on that side would veer off around me. I'd look over the other shoulder and those would veer off the other way. Were they running after me or with me??? If I was sure they were innocently running with me it would be the thrill of a lifetime. But if they were after me, I was in real trouble. And it would only take one! Once I made it to the tree line there was some protection and I felt reasonably safe. It was an amazing experience that I would not care to try again on purpose.

There were cattle in neighboring pastures and the fly population at the new farm was just as bad as it was at home. We had tried hanging long rubs between trees and soaking them with mineral oil containing a fly repellent. It helped a little in stopping those annoying face flies that carried the pink eye virus. The rubs were quickly cut to shreds by the enthusiastic rubbing of horns. However there was a little bullet rub that hung straight down loosely that they could not destroy so easily. It was cheaper, easy to hang, just as effective and the buffalo had great fun playing with it. We used mineral oil as a base for the repellent rather then diesel gas as it was gentler on the animals face.

The first auction that we took animals to that fall was the Oklahoma sale where we had bought the first seven Georges last year. We were returning five of them and also some bull calves including Fridays little guy Rusty. He was cute as could be but still quite small. Pinky was a rancher we had bought some of the calves from last year and I was surprised when he came up to tell me that he was thinking of buying one of my calves. I happily told him all about the various animals we had brought, but when it came time to bid, he bought little Rusty.

Now Pinky was a little fellow himself and he liked little Rusty's personality.
A couple of years after Rusty went home with Pinky, I learned that the two of them were real buddies and Rusty would come to greet him when he came out to visit the herd, although none of the rest of his herd did that. And a few years after that, a fellow at an auction told me he had been visiting Pinky and was told the fine breeding bull in that herd had come from our farm. Rusty had grown up big time!

I was usually on hand to answer questions people might have before the sale and overheard people talking about my animals in the pens. I had to laugh. They had discovered something very different about the buffalo from Oakcreek. Their horns were glistening black while all the other people's buffalo had dull, dry gray looking horns in comparison. It was the mineral oil from the fly rub and they really did look fantastic!

We had not had enough room in the trailer to take all the animals to a single sale. By going to two different sales, we could get double experience and could work fewer animals at one time through the new equipment. That was a learning experience as well. When buffalo get confined they go berserk. They are wild animals and do not tolerate being confined or handled. Its intimidating. Even these little guys bang into the bars and bloody their noses and can even break their necks. When they get too wound up, you have to back off and let them settle or risk serious injury or even death.

We were taking these babes to the Kansas sale in mid November. It happened to be on Leon's birthday. I snuck a birthday cake into the truck, not easy without him finding it, and brought that cake into the buyers reception. He was 72 years old and got lots of attention from folks, even wished a happy Birthday over the loud speaker the next day.

It was hard to say goodbye to my buffalo babes. They were my first grandchildren. I brought along Solo's pan with the rope on it that I used to give her treats with and used it to give treats to our babes in the sale pen. They behaved so well and looked so good that I was quite proud. My friend from Texas bought Solo's boy because he was the only buffalo in the pens that actually came toward her rather than running away. She sent me a letter a few weeks later telling me that what ever we were doing, keep doing it. My grandson buffey was as healthy as could be while the others from the sale had all gotten sick. He also was so calm that he calmed the others down as well.

Sweet Pea was the only heifer we brought to the sale. If we had a crystal ball to know how high she would sell for and what would happen the following year to prices, we would have brought all the girls to sell. Brian Ward was a broker sitting in the arena bidding $2200 for heifer calves for Ted Turner and others. If you wanted a particular animal, you had to get to that price before he did. Sweet Pea sold for $2500, one of five out of over 300 heifer calves who brought that price. Her buyer sent me the nicest letter after the sale saying how fine she was and he knew how much she meant to me, that she would always have a special place in his heart. These two letters were the only ones I ever received like that after a sale, but they really made my heart proud.

It was late in the evening when Leon and I were returning home on the freeway south of Kansas City pulling an empty trailer. I was driving and passed a semi truck. When the trucker flashed his lights at me, I thought he was telling me that it was safe to pull over in front of him. But as I was leaving him far behind me, he continued to flash his lights. It was strange but he was obviously trying to tell me something. I took the next exit and pulled up to the gas pump. Might as well check as I would need gas soon.

When we got out, it was obvious there was fire somewhere. A check of the engine showed nothing wrong and the trailer was fine. The smoke was coming from under the back of the truck. We looked under there and found the spare time happily burning away right below the gas tank. And I had just pulled up next to a gas pump. Running into the station I begged a fire extinguisher and ran back. A trucker took the extinguisher from my hands and put out the fire, then climbed under the truck to remove the tire.

Truckers can be such heros. Without their help who knows what might have happened to us that night. It still give me nightmares. My little brother, a trucker, had always told me that if I ever needed help to ask a trucker. I'm passing that advice along to you. They are the knights of the road.

We went to the National Bison Association Gold Trophy Show and Sale in Denver in January and dreamed of some day showing animals in that sale. One problem with that idea was the snow. The thought of driving all the way to Denver pulling a trailer through snow put a dagger of fear through my heart.

One of the main speakers at the conference the day before the sale was talking about the importance of 'training' your buffalo to be worked so they would not be fearful. To show how 'trainable' a buffalo could be, he showed slides of a little bull he had trained down in Texas the week before. It took the little guy just an hour to be taught to go and touch what ever the speaker pointed at. My friend who had bought Solo's calf turned around in her chair to tell me that my little bull was the one in the slides. Bless his heart, he is famous.

Chapter 13   New bull for a New Herd

When we sold calves for the first time, we could not part with Prince George. He was Eve's son and she is our dominant cow. And Gorgeous George is such a fine father, Prince promises to be an outstanding breeding bull. He did not go to auction. We intended to eventually have him as an apprentice under his own father.

Echo with Prince George, future Monarch of our herd.

We were wading through the ins and outs of line breeding verses inbreeding. We boiled the complicated subject down to a couple of rules to follow. First a full brother and sister should never breed as that would result in inbreeding with bad recessive genes being allowed to come forward. Second, the best way to improve breeding stock through line breeding would be to breed a daughter back to the father. That way if you have an outstanding bull, you would increase his genetics in the offspring.

Keeping Gorgeous George and our original girls meant that there would be no inbreeding or line breeding. Hummmm Well, line breeding would improve the genetics. With the new herd we could use Prince to breed his half sisters to improve the herd – as long as we did not keep a full sister of his. Complicated, but not impossible to work with. On the other hand, if anything happened to Gorgeous George, Prince would still be with us as a replacement. If he bred his mother, it would be line breeding to increase her fine genetics in the herd. OK, I think I understand the concepts now. But Prince has already been sent to the new farm with the other calves and he has no full sisters there. Let him take over that herd for now.

Oh, no, that really does not work. Some of the girls we moved were old enough to breed and Prince is not yet old enough. We need a new bull. Where are we going to get one? We did some research and found some really interesting bulls available in Utah. That's a long way to go to buy a bull. Well, the owner said he was bringing animals to Denver to the Gold Trophy Sale and we were going there also. That helped except that we did not want to drive to Denver with a trailer in January's winter weather.

Arrangements were made for a Missouri ranch who was selling animals in Denver to bring home our new bull in their then empty trailer. We still had to drive across the state to bring the bull home, but it was a lot closer and we could make the trip when we knew the weather would be good.

Quannah was very dark and his babies were beautifully black. He also sang to the ladies when he courted them. He was very gentle for a bull.

It was a little scary to buy a bull based on pictures and pedigrees but it turned out just fine. We christened the handsome fellow Quannah after the Comanche chief Quannah Parker. I had recently read about Quannah, the son of a white captive who became Comanche as she grew up. His father was a Comanche Chief. Quannah was the last Comanche War Chief to surrender. When he finally did surrender, he led his tribe in the transition to their new world. He learned English, became a successful rancher and politician and so on, yet kept all of his Comanche wives, dress and customs. He successfully had a foot in both worlds. I hoped our new bull would do the same, keep his wild buffalo ways yet lead our new herd to success on the farm.

In order to get Quannah settled with his new herd, we put him in the corral with a couple of fine buffalo girls to keep him company. The next time we went to check on the herd, he and the girls were no longer confined. They had broken through the fence to join the herd. I was not happy with this situation until I found the rottweiler dog lying in the barn, still alive but clearly dying. He had attacked the wrong buffalo and had been kicked for his misbehavior. Prince was not real happy about this new boss, but they enjoyed wrestling together.

When summer rolled around, Prince started getting in trouble. There was a wooden picket fence across the pasture near the road where a mobile home used to be. It was pretty marginal as a fence, neither high nor strong enough. We knew it should be replaced but had never gotten around to it.

We got a call from our neighbor who had a small general store about 8 or 10 miles on down the highway. She said a lady stopped in and said 'You won't believe this, there are wild buffalo in Missouri. One chased me down the road."

It was Prince. He was jumping that picket fence and chasing cars down the highway like a dog. We went out to check on the situation but when Prince saw our car coming his way, he went and jumped back over the fence pretending to be innocent.

If we didn't do something fast, it was just a matter of time before his feet tweaked the fence and knocked it over. Or maybe some of the others might decide to start jumping too. Not good either way.

It was a couple days yet before we could get that fence replaced and Prince got in plenty of mischief in the meantime. One man who was forced to stop yelled profanity at the neighbor across the road, but was told "Those aren't my buffalo and if you talk to the owner like you did to me, he's going to stomp a mud hole in you." We never heard from that gentleman. But the lady who reported the 'wild buffalo' told me he was running right along beside her car at 50 miles an hour. I don't think he could go that fast, but he obviously was fast enough to get her attention.

The neighbor stopped me on the dirt road to the farm that fall and said he had not been able to stop and close the gate this time because he was pulling the trailer behind. Seems he had already closed the buffalo's gate a day or two before. There was a padlock on the gate, but we didn't actually lock it, just made it look locked. School had started and older kids apparently thought it would be funny to let the bison out. I staked out the gate in wait the next two mornings, hoping to video the culprits with no luck. It was easier to just lock the gate.

None of the girls at the new farm were old enough to have a calf that summer but here at the house there would be plenty of babes again. And again I would be haunting the herd to be there for the miracle of birth if possible. Lolita and her sister Leona had their first calves. Leona would not accept her calf and just left it behind. I took it back to the herd on the ATV a couple of times, but Leona never accepted it and none of the other cows would let her babe suckle either. It was heart breaking to watch. I finally gave up and took her to the house to bottle feed. Unfortunately, I had waited too long to get colostrum to her. I should have given it to her before trying to take her back to the herd. Holly had no immunity from infections.

Holly was more than happy to take the bottle from me, and later from anyone else who wanted that experience. Soon there was a pen for her by the house made from portable pipe panels and the stock trailer was incorporated into that pen so that she could get in there out of bad weather. Friends came by to erect a shade made out of a tarp so that she could get out of the sun but still be on the grass. A giant white teddy bear was donated to keep her company.

Buffalo don't like to be alone and we had become her herd. I made a bed in the stock trailer for both of us and would put her to bed there in the evening. I would fall asleep with her in the trailer but during the night would wake and steal away to my own bed in the house. It was a joy to be so close to this beautiful buffalo babe and care for her.

It took about a week before the infections began to set in and the flies to become a torment. We tried to keep her little rear end as clean as possible and use fly repellent to keep those terrible pests away. Doc France gave us antibiotics to add to her milk to try to keep her feeling better. It soon became obvious that she was getting sicker by the day and at the end of the second week she had to be in the animal hospital on an IV.

Holly came home from the animal hospital with instructions to keep her in the house where the temperature could be stable. Her little pen was now the entry hallway where the floor could be kept clean. I stayed by her side trying to give her as much comfort as I could and slept beside her all that night. A neighbor had told me that as long as her nose was warm, she would be OK, but if her nose was cold she was dying. I used my hands to try to keep that little nose from getting cold but it was no use. By morning Holly was dead.

When we lose the ones we love, time has a way of healing broken hearts and allowing us to regain the joy of having had them in our lives. Holly was a precious little being and now it is a bittersweet memory that I share with you. I am grateful to have had her with me and have learned from the experience to better care for any future buffalo children that become my responsibility.

It seemed like we waited forever for our first calves and now just when we had gotten to know the calves we saved for the new herd, here were calves bursting out everywhere. I loved it. It was a busy life for us with our woodworking business and two buffalo herds to keep up with. It was fun to attend the Missouri Bison Association meetings and the conferences the National Bison Association put on, plus the auctions. We sure didn't want to miss the auctions. And that time was rolling around again.

I had had it with Lolita. She was getting bolder and bolder with her attacks on the Trooper and stalking me on the ATV. This is spite of the fact that she had a little bull calf to take care of. He would go to auction this fall and Lolita would go with him. When you buy older animals at auction, its always a worry why they were being sent away. In Lolita's case it was important to let people know it was her personality. She didn't need to end up in another small herd yet would likely be just fine in a larger herd with little human interaction.

The sale bill at the Kansas Assn Auction clearly listed that she was being sold because she chased the ATV. When it was her turn to sell, people laughed at her personality problem and because she looked great and was a proven breeder brought $2500. A couple of years later I ran into the rancher who bought her. He reminded me of the cow he bought and said "you should have seen what she did to my pickup!" He had sold her for $1000 and was happy to have her gone. An animal like that needs to be eaten rather than bred. She could affect the behavior of other members of the herd as well and compound the problems she causes.

When winter rolled around this year and we had to put out hay to the herd, Leon had to drive the tractor all the way down Little Missouri Hollow and out on Hwy 90. It was a long, cold drive and there was not as much grazing still available that winter. Once when Leon was unable to get feed out to the new farm, Jamey, who we got our hay from, actually delivered a bale of hay all that distance so the animals could be fed. One of the advantages of living on a farm is that friends and neighbors come to each others aid when troubles come.

The farm across the road from our house had a mobile home in one corner with the rest of the property being farmland with some woods. Our friend Harold owned it and offered to sell it to us. That was hard to pass up. It would be so much easier to look after the herd if it was right across the road. We bought a seven year option to purchase the farm without the mobile home corner and were given the right to improve the fences and use the property during that time. We put our lake house up for sale to help with the purchase price and began fencing and cross fencing the property with electric fencing.

Electric was easier to put up but a lot more of a challenge to maintain. Because Leon and I were doing the work ourselves, we went with easier to put up. I pulled miles of high tensile fence wire that year while Leon managed spooling it out, then came to get me at the other end of that fence run with the ATV. When I was in the woods along the rock bluffs it was pretty scary.... you know, snakes, spiders, ticks and who knows what else. But when we finished most of the pastures we were pretty proud of ourselves.

Our friends from Arkansas, Mike and Janie, helped us fence the first two areas in exchange for using it that year to feed out some of their meat bulls. I sold some of our heifer calves that year and one of the McDaniel's bulls to breed them. We were learning that you did not have to take the buffalo to auction to sell them. It would be easier on us and the animals to sell them from the farm when we could.

There was a lot of discussion among bison producers on the best way to finish, that is to feed them the last few months or more, before processing bison. Cattle are usually put on full feed – lots of grain – and those ranchers thought that made the meat more tender and taste better, and the animals grow faster. The other ranchers thought it was better to not feed grain. The bison did not grow quite as fast or be quite as big at slaughter age, but animals and therefore their meat would be healthier – and they thought taste as good – if not better. We were no longer feeding grain in the form of range cubes to our herd. I take that back, we were feeding them only as treats for a management tool to get them to come when we needed them.

The trade off for having smaller animals at processing time was that grass fed herds required less expense for food and labor. Mike and Janie opted to grain feed their herd. We decided not to. That left us freer to travel and work. With my degree in health education, I was really serious about having healthy food. Mike and Janie also have built a visitors center on their farm with a snack bar selling bison chili, hot dogs and hamburger. We had not taken any animals for meat yet. It was time.

A reporter was interviewing us shortly after we got the girls and had asked us if we ate buffalo meat. My happy reply was that we enjoyed eating buffalo meat but eating one of our girls 'would be like putting the dog in the microwave. We couldn't do it.' And those fifteen girls would always be safe from being eaten. But we now had some calves that had grown big enough for processing and it only made sense to have our own healthy meat.

We chose Harold, one of our calves but one I had not grown attached to. This was at the new farm. We had to move all calves over there because there was not enough room to keep any at home unless we were replacing one that had died. Arrangements were made for a professional to come to the farm to kill and dress the animal and then take it to the processing plant for us. Half the animal was sold to a friend and he was on hand when we put the animal down. Also with us was the tenant of our hundred year old farmhouse. He had a restaurant a mile down the road where it met the highway and was quite interested in how meat was produced.

I put range cubes in the corral and opened the gate for the herd to come in. Any time Harold tried to come in, I spooked him to turn away. Soon all were in the pen but Harold. With everything ready, I put a pile of range cubes on the ground for Harold. He was quite appreciative of the treats and was feasting happily. He looked up our way and BANG. He never knew what hit him. There was no suffering or even surprise. He dropped to his knees and onto his side. It was a strange feeling to watch even though it was carefully planned and executed.

We watched as the entrails were removed and the hide. That hide was going to a friend who would tan it and also would make the skull into a work of art. The herd paid no attention to what was going on outside their pen. They saw it and looked our way but their eyes did not linger long. It was not upsetting for them. When they were released from the pen, they did check out the place where the entrails were waiting for the buzzards and varmints to clean up. It was curiosity, not recognition.

The restaurant owner took a prime rib cut back to the Shrimpman's Inn where he was preparing a delicious dinner for us to appreciate eating our own meat for the first time. It was a fitting occasion. Processing our first animal was a milestone.

A few months later we were hosting a buffalo field day for other bison ranchers and people who were interested in raising bison. On the menu for lunch that day was Bison Lasagna A LA Harold. I gave this short presentation and blessing before the meal that day.

Six years ago, Mike Surbrugg from the Joplin Globe came out here to our farm. We had just gotten our first 15 buffalo girls. In his interview, Mike asked us about eating buffalo. We told him happily that we ate buffalo meat, but i said that eating one of our own would be kind of like "putting the dog in the microwave".

Living on a farm for 6 years has given me a new perspective and understanding of where our food comes from. We are all here today because we love buffalo. But few of us could afford to raise many buffalo without an economic return for our efforts. And even someone like Ted Turner cannot continue to keep all the offspring of their herd indefinitely. The economic return from raising buffalo is in selling meat. If we give the responsibility of selling that meat to others, then they will also claim the profits. And soon their share of the profits will increase until we are unlikely to cover the costs of production from the price they pay us for the animals.

This year we held back bull calves for the purpose of starting meat sales. When I announced to friends that we would be slaughtering a bull for meat for the first time, my friends were concerned about how I would handle the experience. Many of you here have never had that experience either, and would undoubtedly ask yourself that same question. So I would like to share with you how I felt about butchering our first animal.

My first reaction was one of "awe". When the bull fell to his knees, I felt a strong sense of respect for the sacrifice that this young bull made in order that his herd would survive and prosper. It has enabled me to understand my own place in nature, and my own position in the food chain in which all living things are a part. I feel a great appreciation for the nourishment this animal provides my own body that I might survive. I feel that now he lives again as a part of me and of many others. There is a new feeling of kinship with the Native Americans whose lives depended so strongly on the buffalo. They called him Brother Buffalo.

Today that buffalo becomes a part of you also. I would like to share with you my own prayer of thanksgiving to Brother Buffalo.

I EAT YOU BECAUSE I LOVE YOU MY BROTHER. I BECOME A PART OF YOU, AS YOU BECOME A PART OF ME.

Chapter 14   Auction Prices Drop

Auction time rolled around again come fall and Leon and I had brought a trailer load of calves to the Kansas Sale. As always, the social part of the event was special and everyone was excited to sell their animals. For many it would be the sole payday for a year's worth of work and planning. The bleachers were full and everyone waited for the first animal to come into the ring.

The clanging doors opened and in came a beautiful heifer calf who had been chosen by the judges to be the best of show. Bidding opened on what should have been the highest selling heifer at the sale. No one bid. The auctioneer dropped the asking price to $300 and got a bid and then went to $400. Yes. Do I hear $500, silence. Finally going once, going twice SOLD for $400. There was a stunned silence in the room. Everyone had expected her to sell for at least $2000.

While the audience tried to wrap their heads around the price of the first girl, a second was let into the ring. Do I hear $300? Yes. Do I hear $400? Silence. Soon she was sold for $300. Another came into the ring. Do I hear $300? Silence. Do I hear $250? Yes. Do I hear $275? Yes. Do I hear $300. Silence. SOLD $275.

There was a deadly silence throughout the arena as shock set in. Ranchers were depending on this paycheck to meet their bills. They had paid big money for their breeding stock and had never expected this. Faces were looking stricken. I whispered to Leon that we could sell our calves and bring home the best of the show for very little money. He shook his head NO. We'll take them back home unless they bring a minimum of at least $300. Mature cows ended the auction, a couple hundred of them, and sold for $200 each. We were returning home with half our calves.

This is what America must have been like during the depression as citizens tried to survive the hard times. I had never experienced any situation remotely like this. What should we do? We had bought more land and increased our herds. We were on schedule to purchase the farm across the road where we were working on fencing. Should we go through with that? One thing for sure, at this point I never wanted to take an animal to auction ever again.

Looking at our options, we decided to continue to expand our herd with the calves on hand rather than sell them for such low prices. We set rock bottom price for our calves at $500 for now to let go of any of them. And we would sell meat. We didn't have the slightest idea of how to go about selling meat but we could learn. And we could hope for the best and that prices would rebound.

Everyone was trying to determine what had happened to the market. Prices had been driven up by some specific things. Big buyers had invested heavily in starting herds, but were now selling animals that did not work for their operations plus the calves they were producing. The Canadian government had spurred bison sales with government financing which was now coming to an end. The North American Bison Co-operative had started up in North Dakota and guaranteed a market in that area for bison. Members had to provide bulls for processing for each share and they had needed heifer calves to start their herds, spurring competition for the available calves. Now they had their herds and the bull calves they needed and were selling heifer calves rather than buying. It was a deadly bottle neck to the bison industry.

The Missouri Bison Association website had a website membership page where folks could locate producers who might have meat or animals for sale. They hosted booths at the State Fair and Farmfest. With a membership cost of only $35 a year, it was good advertising for its members. As newsletter editor, I put together a color brochure for the organization. It featured pictures of my herd, without giving recognition as such, because those were the photos that were available.

In order help improve the market for bison by increasing meat sales, we decided to produce a cookbook called Cooking With American Buffalo. A working committee was formed and teamwork was outstanding. Within six months it was at the printer featuring 300 recipes, a custom painting on the cover and lots of information about bison and their meat.

Two thousand copies were printed and a list price of $6.95 was set. It has subsequently been reprinted two more times at 2000 copies each time. Printing costs went up, increasing the price to $10. Volume discounts are still available and it remains a good seller. Readers learn more than they could ask for about why eat bison – which by the way is the same thing as American buffalo. Here is nutrition information for you from the cookbook. Some of the information below was added for visitors to my own website and is marked.

About Buffalo Meat

HEALTHY CHOICE: Meat does not get any healthier than Bison meat, unless it is free-range, grass-fed American Buffalo. You probably know already that Bison and American Buffalo are simply different names for the same animal. Which name you choose is up to you.

COOKING WITH BUFFALO: Cooking with buffalo is easy! This delicious red meat can be substituted in any recipe used for beef, with just a few adjustments. For one thing it cooks faster, and gets you out of the kitchen sooner. Here you can learn how to adjust your cooking methods for the low fat cooking of Buffalo meat.

RECIPES: You know your favorite family meals, and we hope you will not hesitate to try Buffalo meat in your own recipes.

HEALTHY CHOICE
America's Original Health Food

If you are concerned about your health and want to eat food that is good for you - and yet not sacrifice taste and flavor for better nutrition - then buffalo is the meat for you. Sweet, flavorful and tender, buffalo meat still packs a nutritional wallop. Exceptionally high in protein and minerals, bison is low in fat, calories and cholesterol. It tends to satisfy you more while eating less.

The American Heart Association recommends bison meat for a heart healthy diet due to its low fat and cholesterol content. Buffalo is high in protein, iron, selenium, phosphorus, zinc, copper, potassium, riboflavin, niacin, and vitamins B6 and B12. Its more than heart healthy - Its PEOPLE HEALTHY.

Meat	Fat Grams	Calories	Cholesterol
Bison	2.42	143	82
Chicken	7.41	190	89
Beef	9.3	211	86
Pork	10.5	215	92

USDA Handbook per 100 gram serving (just over 3 ounces)

Bison grazing on green grass have a very healthy fat. Omega 3 fatty acids and CLA (conjugated nucleic acid) help in controlling weight and fighting cancers, among other properties. These fatty acids are deficient in most American diets. Feeding grain to animals lessens the amount of these fats. It must be kept in mind, however, that bison meat is lean, and not considered a high source of fat whether from grass or from grain. Many producers chose to add some grain to the finishing diet of bison to produce meat with a consistent flavor as the grass varies with the seasons and the location.

While listing all the benefits IN bison meat, we shouldn't forget what is NOT IN the meat. In addition to having fewer calories, less fat and less cholesterol, there are no growth hormones, steroids, or sub-therapeutic antibiotics. These animals are both environmentally friendly and people friendly.

Bison meat is versatile and satisfying, easy to prepare, and can be used in any recipe requiring beef. Give your health and taste buds a treat, and eat BUFFALO, America's Original Health Food.

More Information About Bison Nutrition

At the August 2002 meeting of the Missouri Bison Association, nutritionist Barbara Lohse Knouse, PHD, RD, LD from Kansas State University spoke about the nutritional value of bison meat. Dr. Knouse feels that there are many important advantages to bison meat in addition to "High in protein, Low in fat and Low in Cholesterol". This is especially important during this time when more people are pursuing healthier nutritional lifestyles.
Dr. Knouse highlighted the following advantages of bison nutrition:

B6 and B12 (Bison is a HIGH of these vitamins)
Vitamin B12 is only available from animal sources
Vitamin B12 has been shown to keep the elderly mentally alert
Vitamin B6 is needed for protein metabolism

Sodium (Bison is a LOW source of Sodium)
High sodium intake is associated with hypertension

Potassium (Bison is a HIGH source or Potassium)
Key to lowering Blood Pressure
Most foods high in potassium are also high in calories
Bison contains 1/3 more potassium than chicken

Iron (Bison is a HIGH source of Iron)
Necessary for hemoglobin formation and prevention of anemia.
Bison is 3 times higher in Iron than pork or chicken.

Selenium (Bison is a HIGH source of Selenium)
An antioxidant shown to help prevent cancer.
Bison has 4 times higher amount of Selenium than the USDA recommends as an antioxidant.

Conjugated Linoleic Acid (Bison is a high source of CLA)
Antioxidant that has been shown to help prevent cancer

Calories (Bison is a LOW source of calories) 1/2 the calories of pork and chicken

Dr. Knouse emphasized the huge differences between American Buffalo (Bison) meat and Water Buffalo meat. In her research, when a NUTRITION LABEL stated only "Buffalo", it referred to Water Buffalo. American Buffalo meat is labeled "Bison", not "Buffalo" in NUTRITION CHARTS.

My View on Why Grass Finished Meat is Healthy

Many people associate grain feeding of animals with both taste and health. The fact is, just the opposite is true. Bison did not evolve eating grain, and it is not a natural healthy diet for them.

WHAT MAKES GRASS-FINISHED MEAT SO SPECIAL??

That's easy! Its better for:

**the animals- When allowed to range freely, buffalo enjoy a twilight grazing session. They like to graze in the early evening because the temperature is more moderate, the flies are less persistent, and the grass tastes sweeter. Now doesn't that sound better than a dusty feedlot? And their diet is a whole lot healthier for them as well.*

**the consumer- Products from pastured animals are ideal for human health. Very similar to wild game, they contain the amounts and kinds of nutrients that our bodies "expect" to be fed. The research suggests that switching to grassfed products may reduce the risk of a number of diseases, including diabetes, obesity, cardiovascular disease, and cancer.*

**the environment- New studies show that raising animals on pasture is not only less harmful to the ecosystem than raising animals in confinement, it may offer net benefits. Natural grasslands can be just as effective at sequestering carbon dioxide as forests.*

** the farm family - Farmers who raise their animals on pasture enjoy a number of benefits including being able to raise their families in a peaceful environment and eat nutritious, all-natural food. They are also spared the health hazards associated with factory farming. Just as important, many farmers are able to make a living selling their pastured products directly to consumers or restaurants. As the public becomes more aware of the benefits of pastured products, thousands of small family farms may survive*

Many growers who grain feed and grain finish will list their animals as grass-fed. And they are! They get hay, and may even have access to pasture. But if they are fed grain it changes the fat composition of the animal. Other livestock producers may list their meat as organically grown. That usually means that the grain the animals receive is organically grown, and does not promise you that the animals are NATURALLY raised on grass. That's why you should ask if the animal is GRAIN-FINISHED or GRASS-FINISHED.

When you switch from grain-fed to grass-finished meat, it provides you with a wealth of health benefits. You avoid all those extra layers of high cholesterol fats, the synthetic hormones, antibiotics, pesticide residues, and other additives found in feed lot animals. But even more importantly, with grass-finished animals you get some wonderful nutritional advantages: MORE OMEGA-3 FATTY ACIDS, CLA, BETA CAROTENE, AND A WHOLE LOT FEWER CALORIES. You are saying "OK, I'll take your word for it", because you do not know what that means? The answers could fill a book - or a website. That's just what Jo Robinson has done at eatwild.com. If you don't find enough information here, I suggest that you explore eatwild.com for more.

*****OMEGA-3 FATTY ACIDS fatty acids are not only good for your health, they are essential for normal growth and development. Furthermore, you can't manufacture them in your body, so you must get them from your diet. This is why omega-3 fatty* acids are one the the few fats to be classified as "essential fatty acids." Most Americans consume a diet with inadequate supplies of Omega-3.

Many growers who grain feed and grain finish will list their animals as grass-fed. And they are! They get hay, and may even have access to pasture. But if they are fed grain it changes the fat composition of the animal. Other livestock producers may list their meat as organically grown. That usually means that the grain the animals receive is organically grown, and does not promise you that the animals are NATURALLY raised on grass. **That's why you should ask if the animal is GRAIN-FINISHED or GRASS-FINISHED.**

When you switch from grain-fed to grass-finished meat, it provides you with a wealth of health benefits. You avoid all those extra layers of high cholesterol fats, the synthetic hormones, antibiotics, pesticide residues, and other additives found in feed lot animals. But even more importantly, with grass-finished animals you get some wonderful nutritional advantages: MORE OMEGA-3 FATTY ACIDS, CLA, BETA CAROTENE, AND A WHOLE LOT FEWER CALORIES.

You are saying "OK, I'll take your word for it", because you do not know what that means? The answers could fill a book - or a website. That's just what Jo Robinson has done at eatwild.com. If you don't find enough information here, I suggest that you explore eatwild.com for more.

****OMEGA-3 FATTY ACIDS 3 fatty acids are not only good for your health, they are essential for normal growth and development. Furthermore, you can't manufacture them in your body, so you must get them from your diet. This is why omega-3 fatty acids are one the the few fats to be classified as "essential fatty acids." Most Americans consume a diet with inadequate supplies of Omega-3.

****CLA stands for Conjugated Linoleic Acid, another "good fat". Ruminant animals are the richest known source of this substance. Although the research is in its earliest stages, CLA shows promise of reducing the risk of cancer, obesity, diabetes, and a number of immune disorders . What's more, CLA appears to be perfectly safe. Even in very large doses, this good fat has shown no harmful effects in laboratory animals. That's what makes these "good fats" as opposed to the artery clogging "bad fats" associated with grain.

Chapter 15   Back from the Brink

Learning to sell meat at the farm was pretty intimidating. In order to sell meat by the pound from the farm did not really require that it be inspected by the USDA the way beef, pork and chicken is done. This is because the meat inspection act did not include bison in the law. But health departments tended not to care about that, they wanted everything inspected to insure it was safe. USDA was quite willing to inspect our animals – for a price. Since they were not required to provide the inspection, they charged for doing it. It was expensive and added to the price we would have to charge for the meat.

Another expense that I ran into was getting labels approved by USDA and having them printed. The nearest USDA inspected facility willing to process bison proved to be in Branson, a two and a half hour drive each way. I waited while the animals were processed so that I could bring the heads home. I usually left the hide as it was too much work to salt and store hides without a market for them. A whole day and plenty of expense was involved in getting the animals to the processor.

About ten days later, I would make the same trip to pick up the frozen processed meat. All these factors increased the cost of the meat in comparison with the big processing companies for beef with their adjacent feedlots. And those feedlots provided the beef processors both convenience and profit by putting weight, much of it fat, on the animals waiting to be processed. Farms selling their own meat could not compete with the lower costs of processing meats by the big companies.

There were a couple of smaller processors closer to me that were inspected, but they had bad experiences or had heard horror stories about trying to process bison. I made repeated stops at Clouds Meats in Carthage trying to get them to process my animals as it was a really impressive place. There was a glut of bison meat on the market as the prices of live animals dropped and the meat prices were depressed as well. Because it was unique and not readily available everywhere, we were still able to sell at prices exceeding beef.

There were some in the farm to table market who wanted to be able to process and sell their own meat products on the farm without going through the inspection process. I was not a part of this movement. For me, let the experts at processing handle that part, and let me concentrate on what I love best, raising animals and selling meat. I joined the discussion on inspections in a article published in the Stockman Grassfarmer in October of 2001 which was subsequently reprinted in two other publications.

"The Case for an Expanded Meat Inspection Service"

Pineville, Missouri: Food safety is something most Americans take pretty much for granted. We can thank the fine work of the Food Safety Inspection Service, through the USDA and the FDA for this protection and peace of mind. Few of us would be willing to trade this safety in order to improve the quality of our food. We should no have to. We have a right to both food safety and food quality.

While I do not want to seem unappreciative for the efforts of the Inspection Service, the truth of the matter is that we pay dearly for the food safety we enjoy. The cost to our communities, our health and our finances can be difficult to measure, but are none the less staggering.

In the August 2001 issue of the Stockman Grassfarmer, Joel Salatin advised us that market access is the fundamental issue faced by environmentally friendly agriculture, family farms, and rural enterprises. This is nothing new.

From the inception of the inspection program, the small producer and processor was locked out of the retail market. The result was the disappearance of the family farm and the disintegration of the rural communities. It was one of the first costs of the food safety programs.

Today's farmers are becoming contract labor for the large processing companies. Why? The inspection process has created a bottle-neck which gives undue control of both the processing facilities and market access to only a very few companies. The inspection service is concerned with food safety rather than food quality. If we look at the issues of food quality, we can see some of the problems that result from confinement 'factory farming'

In the beef industry, feedlots owned by the processing plant can manage supply, while at the same time increasing their profits. But confining large numbers of animals in crowded facilities results in disease. To counter this, sub-therapeutic levels of antibiotics are routinely fed to these animals.

Feedlot operators have also found that one of the most cost effective methods of adding weight to the animals is through hormone implants, subjecting the consumer to the long term effects of this practice.

Then consider the increase in fat composition of those feedlot animals. As we consume that fat, we become fatter also. One of the few 'quality issues' that the inspection service does address is the grading of meat. This fat, well marbled meat gets their highest endorsement.

This fatty meat simply is not healthy for human consumption. As a result, nutritionists advise their patients to limit their meat consumption. Out of fear of this some people stop eating meat altogether.

But life is not so simple. Farming practices have depleted non-meat foods of much of their nutritional content, and eye-appeal is their most dominant quality.

The fact is that fat is necessary for our survival. The question is how much and what kind? Nutrients such as CLA and Omega-3 fatty acids actually improve our health. But you will not find enough in these feedlot beef. It takes grass to produce a 'healthy meat'.

In many parts of the country, milk is produced in confinement daries. Thousands of cows are milked each day in these daries and they never see a blade of grass. So much for 'healthy' milk. Hormone implants in these dairy cows provide increases in milk production and further diminishes the quality of that milk available to consumers.

A neighbor contracts poultry for one of the big guys. I asked him if it was really true the feed supplied by that company contains arsenic to stimulate the bird's appetite. He told me that it is also there to help prevent disease in the confined chickens. But not to fear, they stop feeding it before slaughter. So I had to wonder - if they process the birds at three months and they feed arsenic to grow, just when do they take this poison out of the food? And how much of it remains in the meat that we eat? Does arsenic in our food stimulate our appetite and does it protect us from disease also?

The public does not perceive that they are paying too high a price for their food. But if costs are measured by the long term expense, it is a different story. What happens if you factor in the medical expenses for treatment of heart disease, diabetes, high blood pressure, cholesterol control and cancer?

What price do we put on the loss of work and the suffering resulting from these health issues? If we add all these costs to the price of inadequate and adulterated foods, we would decide that we can no longer afford to eat.

Is 'food quality' as important as 'food safety'? You bet! But it is the responsibility of the consumer to control. There is no government agency which regulates food quality . And complaining is not going to get the problems erased. We need solutions.

Is there a solution? Joel Salatin is correct that he produces superior quality products , and the consumer should have a right to purchase that food directly from him without interference from bureaucrats. But not every farmer wants to sell their products directly to the consumer. And certainly most of our population does not have direct access to farm products.

It may well be that on farm slaughtering is not the answer. Our long term solution must be greater than that. What we need is to once more have slaughter facilities in our communities, this time complete with inspections. This would improve the economic prosperity of small farms and rural communities. It would also provide access by the public to 'quality food' as well as 'safe food' and improve the the overall health and prosperity of the American consumer.

Put simply, we need to expand this inspection service. Think about tit. If you had one hundred inspected slaughter facilities in your state instead of a dozen, wouldn't one of them likely be close to you? And your business would be important to a local processor.

We need to decide if expanding the inspection service is a good idea, and if so, what is the best way to accomplish this process. The USDA would rather get out of the inspection business than expand it. States are being encouraged to take over the inspection service and over half of the states now have state meat inspection programs. The state inspection requirements must be equal to or grater than USDA requirements.

In January 2001, the State of Missouri began its state meat inspection program. In the months since then four plants began inspections. One of these plants is fifty miles from me, cutting the travel distance to less than half to the nearest plant. That may not be ideal, but it is an improvement.

As you can see, this trend is heading in the direction of rural inspected facilities and can benefit small farms. There are, however, a few problems associated with state inspections. At this time, the state inspected meat cannot cross state lines for sale, and can only be sold within the state.

Meat can now be imported into a state from Mexico, Argentina, Canada, and so forth, but cannot be imported from a neighboring state under a state inspection program. A value added product such as a gourmet sausage, cannot get interstate marketing unless produced in the USDA facility. A bill through Congress will be required to end this discrimination against state inspected products.

The question arises of why a facility would want to be state inspected rather than

USDA if the requirements are the same but the benefits are not. The answer to that question given by the Missouri Department of Agriculture is that they care – about the success of the processor, the farmer, and the economic prosperity of the community. And, yes, they care about food safety also.

Does your state care? Has it invested the effort and expense required to establish an inspection program? The framework is in place for the expansion of the inspection service. But not only do we need the state inspections to be recognized as equal to USDA, we need a stamp that proves the equivalency such as SS-USDA (where SS is replaced by the state abbreviation) to eliminate any doubt as to the safety of the products.

We need to make our voices heard in our state and federal governments that this is a crucial issue to family farms, rural communities and the American public."

OK, I'm off my soap box now but am happy to report that Clouds Meats was the newly state inspected plant near me. Clouds took advantage of the glut to buy a palette load of bison 'trim' - which is ground into burger – from a processor in South Dakota. The Joplin Globe caught wind of the fact that bison was now available in Carthage and did a full front page article. Business soared as people came to try bison and went home with many other meats as well. As they purchased more and more bison, the Clouds began to reconsider processing bison at their facility. That made life much easier for me as they were only an hour away and did a fantastic job.

Each animal I took for processing netted about 400 pounds of boneless meats. It was vacuum sealed in see thru packages and frozen. Clouds was also expert at making jerky, summer sausage, snack sticks and other value add products. With this inventory, I was ready to try my luck at the farmers market in Bentonville, Arkansas fifteen miles away.

A big market umbrella shaded a table for me at the market. It was much easier to set up and take down than a canopy. I could put jerky, snack sticks and summer sausage out for sale on the table. In the van was a freezer that I had to take out and put back each week with frozen cuts of meat. A package of snack sticks and summer sausage was cut into small bite sized pieces for people to taste and information about the nutritional value was put out on the table. Picture albums showed the farm and how the animals were raised. I would be there each Saturday from nine to eleven, maybe longer, but I would not guarantee it.

The freezer turned out to be way too much work for the amount of sales it generated and I soon stopped bringing it. If folks wanted frozen meats, they would have to order it in advance and I would bring it in a cooler. I had little cooler bags make with the farm logo and phone number for people to take their purchases home. The cooler bags were a $3 deposit. I would see my customers coming at the market, swinging their little cooler bags by their sides. It was working well. I invited folks to come to the farm to purchase meat and see the animals. That worked well also.

For two years the farmers market took my Saturday mornings. But the rules changed and you had to be there the full market hours. If you couldn't be there, you had to call so they could give your spot to someone else. And the price went way up as well. It was not worth it. No more farmers market for me.

Surprisingly, so many folks started coming to the farm on a Saturday, I found I sold more at home than I had at the market. And these folks would be year round customers rather than just one day in the summer. They also were loyal to 'their buffalo farm' and brought friends and relatives. Word of mouth was spreading about how good and healthy the meat was and how convenient it was to come to the farm. And it was awesome to see buffalo up close. Selling meat was now easy and fun, and these customers were soon friends.

It was past time to get our own website up and running, but that could be expensive and time consuming. When someone who was a professional web builder wanted to buy buffalo from me to start a small herd, we worked out a trade. He would get two heifer calves in exchange for building the website and teaching me to manage it. He bought a bull calf at the Missouri Bison Assn auction near their farm and would pick up the heifer calves when they also picked up the bull.

These new bison owners had made a pen next to their barn with portable panels and backed the trailer up to the pen. When they opened the door of the trailer the buffalo did not come up. But stepping up on the side of the trailer to look inside was a mistake. A buffalo spooked and came tearing out of the trailer, knocked down a panel of the pen and ran off into the pasture. They managed to get the panel back up before the others got out – but how to get the missing buffalo back?

Thinking that the spooked buffalo would be fine with the horses, they did not worry for now. Unfortunately the horses spooked the poor buffalo bull again and he went through the perimeter fence onto the neighbor's property. That's when I got the call from some pretty upset bison owners. I told them to put a bucket of feed on their side of the fence just inside of the break. Buffalo don't like to be alone and he would probably come back to be with the other two buffalo. The bucket would call attention to the opening to help him find the way back in. It worked like a charm. The next morning he was outside the pen where the two girls were.

Now it was time to make the website. I had written lots of flyers, so had material that could be used and LOTS of pictures. It was fun making the website but somehow I never learned how to manage that website called ourbuffalo.com. After a couple of years, the website went off the internet. It was still intact on the server, but the name now led to a college in New York state. With the help of the server I managed to get back online with the new website name of www.ourbuffalofarm.com. I also taught myself how to add more to the website and change what was on there. It wasn't all that hard and I enjoyed the process.

I was now selling buffalo meat to a health food store at the same price I sold meat at home. The only concession was that I would deliver it and they would have up to a month to pay. I was also delivering to a chef of a small cafe in a large gym. He put a display of my flyer on the counter with a card holder. Any of the gym customers who wanted to buy bison could take a card and come to the farm. These were health conscious folks and a lot of customers came our way from the gym and health food store.

A diet center also provided a lot of customers for the farm to buy meat. Their clients were getting tired of fish and chicken and were happy to be allowed to eat red meats. Soon the diet center was taking orders from their clients and I would deliver six or eight orders at a time. And those folks also got information about coming to the farm for purchases and to see the buffalo.

Selling meat was turning out to be easy after all. The one thing that I had refused to do was pay for advertising the meats. Its too hard to reach the right people and it is expensive. The only exception I made was a listing on www.eatwild.com. This excellent website charged only a one time $25 to be listed as a source of locally grown, grassfed meats. It is a site highly I recommend you to check out for resources near you. I was impressed at how quickly I started getting calls from Eat Wild. Here is more information about that site:

Eatwild was founded in 2001. Its mission was to promote the benefits—to consumers, farmers, animals, and the planet—of choosing meat, eggs, and dairy products from 100% grass-fed animals or other non-ruminant animals fed their natural diets. Eatwild is now the #1 clearinghouse for information about pasture-based farming and features a state-by-state directory of local farmers who sell directly to consumers.

Not content to just spread the word about healthier meat, eggs, and dairy, in 2013 Eatwild founder Jo Robinson published a new book--Eating on the Wild Side--which soon became a NY Times Bestseller. This new book presents 21st century research about the important health benefits of choosing specific varieties of fruits and vegetables, as well as hands-on advice on how to shop for them, grow them, cook them, and store them so that their nutritional value is maintained. Jo gleaned this information by reviewing thousands of research articles, providing a wealth of information you will not find anywhere else. <u>Read more about this prize-winning book...</u>

Today, **Eatwild.com** *provides research-based information about* **"eating on the wild side."** *This means choosing present-day foods that approach the nutritional content of wild plants and game—our original diet. Evidence is growing on an almost daily basis that these wholesome foods give us more of the nutrients we need to fight disease and enjoy optimum health. Few of us will go back to foraging in the wild for our food, but we can learn to forage in our supermarkets, farmers markets, and from local farmers to select the most nutritious and delicious foods available.*

In 2016, the Academy of Culinary Nutrition recognized Jo's contributions to healthier eating by selecting her as one of their <u>Top 50 Food Activists</u>.

I've told you a lot about learning to sell meat, but there is much more to the story. You have to produce that meat before you can sell it. At our farm, that means holding on to some of the calves and letting them stay with the herd until they are big enough. While that is a pleasure, it also is a limit to how many other animals can be kept as breeding stock. Like everything thing else in life, it a trade off. Because I enjoy selling meat and it helps diversify the income for the farm, it works for me.

You are undoubtedly thinking "How can she do that to her children?" It goes back to Harold. I do it because I love them. Farming increases the number of animals by eating them, not reduces them. Most buffalo in the world today are in private herds – producing meat, just like most cows and chickens. Would you want a pig for a pet if you didn't eat bacon? How many pigs would there be in the world if there was no bacon?

But you would be right, it is hard to choose which animal is to be taken from the herd for meat. I'm looking for a bull who is big enough. Only one out of ten bulls gets to be the breeding bull. The job of the other bulls is to support the herd. If there are not two bulls ready when I need meat, I have to look at the females for one that the farm would be better off culling from the herd and replaced with a younger animal. Lolita is an example of a female who would be chosen. It becomes an opportunity to improve the herd as well as providing meats. If you're like me, the choosing is the hard part. I'm always afraid the animals will know what I am thinking. I wrote this 'perspective' to put words to my feelings.

Through Buffalo Eyes

The eyes of the buffalo were warm pools of understanding
when finally I looked into them.
"You're feeling guilty today." they said.
"You are ashamed to look at us.
You are deciding which of us must leave,
and you are afraid we will know your thoughts.
Meat is needed before long and it is we who provide it.
And some must leave to make room for the beautiful heifers
you would like to place into our herd.
"No one lives forever".
We understand that the weakest will leave first.
Each one of us wants to be the strongest,
and we test each other every day.
If you need help in making your decisions,
then ask us.
You will see that they give their lives for a purpose,
and by doing so will provide for those who remain.
That is good. We welcome the daughters
you bring to our herd.
They are the future and our family.
Make your decisions wisely. We depend on you."

Once the decision is made on the animals to be processed, they have to be sorted from the herd. In order to do that with the least disruption to the herd and without trauma to the chosen animal, sorting is a job I do without anyone else around. Range cubes are put in the feeders in the big pen attached to the corral. The gate is closed so the animals can't get in to 'help' me with this task, but I make as much noise as possible to attract the herd's attention. Usually by the time 'lunch is served', the herd is circling the pen like an attack on a wagon train.

When the gate is opened, the herd rushes in and I go out on the ATV as soon as it is clear and close the herd in. They get about an hour or so to eat, then I come back to start the sorting procedure. I open the gate about three feet wide to let them come out at their leisure while I sit behind the gate on the ATV. If the chosen animal nears to come out the gate, I use the ATV to close the opening. That also spooks my target to not want to come near the gate for awhile. Once more the gate is opened for animals to come and go as they please. Eventually every one, or at least most, of the rest of the herd has left the pen. I then open the gate to the corral. They think this is the way out and I can complete the sorting process in the smaller pens and have the animals locked where I need them.

I usually sort the animals a few days to a week ahead of the scheduled visit to the processor. If I wait until the last minute, something would likely go wrong and I would not have time for a second chance. Appointments with the processor are getting harder to schedule all the time and I don't want to mess up. I can also put the trailer at the load out alley and put range cubes in there. With this training, some times the bulls go right in to get the treats and I can just close the trailer door behind them. Other times I need to pressure them into the alley and then the trailer. I usually have help at this point to pull the gate shut at the right moment.

Once the animal is in the trailer there is an hour ride to Carthage to Cloud's Meat Processing. There they are placed in a large grassy pen, almost a small field where they graze in the pasture until the next morning. A rifle shot puts them down and they are moved into the building dangling from a tractor. My job was finished when I let the animals out of the trailer and the processor takes it from there.

I don't go back for the head or hide the next day. After the animal's carcass is cleaned it is hung to age a few days in temperature just above freezing. It is then cut to my specifications in a 'cut list' and vacuum sealed in clear plastic so people can see the cuts of meat. The inspector sees the animal live and watches the cutting process to insure the meat is healthy. The processor prints the approved labels that show the meat has been inspected, is bison, the owner of the animal, where it was processed and when.

Things don't always go as planned. I wrote this article for the bison association newsletter.

RICHCHET by Carol Klein

"It was just a normal phone call, a customer interested in buffalo meat and our farm, how we raise our animals and process the meat. I was happily telling him about the farm, but then the panic came."The reason I'm asking" said the caller, "is that we bought a roast from your farm at the health food store. We cooked it – it was delicious – but as we were eating, my three year old started choking. When we cleared her throat, there was a bullet lodged there. Could someone have shot your buffalo?"

It was the kind of call you get nightmares about. Learning to sell meat is not something that many of us know how to do, and we worry about liability and things like that. I assured the gentleman the animal had been healthy and an inspector had verified that, but that the processor did a field kill with a gun to put the animal down. I would be happy to talk with my processor and get back with you. Turns out that it was most likely a ricochet that went into the chuck cut in the animal's chest.

In my mind's eye, I was picturing the cartridge shell, rather than the ugly lead slug, but that is a girl for you. I called the man back with my report from the processor. His response was "I'm not trying to give you a hard time. I thought you would want to know and I would like to get a replacement roast." As you can imagine, I was more than happy to bring the replacement roast to his fitness center. He gave me a piece of the meat that clearly showed the fresh travel of the bullet through the meat and the slug that had been found. He was very interested in the farm and asked if he could visit the following weekend.

He came with his wife and another couple that weekend and we visited the herd in the beat up buffalo-mobile. They loved the experience. Turns out the other gentleman had a large fitness center in Bentonville with a gourmet cafe inside. I was soon delivering fifty pounds of meat every few weeks to his chef. So one of the first effects of that ricochet was to get me an excellent customer, but it certainly did not end there.

The chef put a display on the counter telling about the buffalo meat and the farm and it had a little pocket for my business cards. I just had to refill the cards each time I made a delivery. Members of the gym who wanted to buy buffalo meat were soon calling and I had lots more customers from the ricochet. One young man who visited the farm for meat rekindled a long held dream of raising buffalo. He and his family came by the farm on day and announced that they had bought a farm and they were going to raise buffalo about twenty minutes away. That young man bought calves from me to start his herd (ricochet) and also went to the MoBA sale for more. He was soon on the board of the bison association.

The gourmet cafe is no longer there, but the young men still come out for meat. I was telling one young man the story of the ricochet the other day and how it had rippled out to touch so many people and that those ripples just keep spreading.

He laughed and told me how those ripples had gone on from him as well. But after he left, I was thinking about those ripples - they did not just spread out to touch other people, they came back to me as well. The ricochet has blessed me in more ways than I can tell you, but especially with the people it has brought into my life.

We know that we affect the lives of others, but it is rare that we can look at a single moment and see how it has affected so many people. And its strange that the ricochet was 'frozen' in a roast for who knows how long before those effects began to spread. And they will continue to ripple out to infinity, more than likely. How many lives have been touched or will be? Is there someone in the far corner of the world whose life will be affected by that ricochet? Could it even change history someday? For many of us it already has.

I think back to the moment of the ricochet and wonder at all the events, people and decisions that went into putting the bison in front of that bullet. If any of those things had not happened, my life and the lives of so many others would be different. If the little girl had been injured when she choked on that slug, it would have been very unfortunate. But the ripples created from that point on have been, without exception as far as I can tell, all positive. The world is richer and more interesting because that bullet ricocheted. I believe that the reason for good effects are due to the positive attitudes and respect shared by people, starting with the father of that little girl.

The bison industry is a close community and how we interact is crucial for our success. If we work together and reach out to help one another, we will all be the better off. But what really brings us together is the bison. Our success is theirs as well. I hope each one of you will reach out in a positive way and create all the ripples you can."

Chapter 16   Health Issues

One of the very first things we were told about bison was that they were strong, hardy animals that rarely got sick. That is undoubtedly true in a wild, free-range habitat, however when they are pastured in what is not their natural environment they are subject to diseases of cattle and other animals as well.

Pinkeye is a good example of this. When buffalo grazed over vast plains they left their manure behind them to fertilize the soil. And with that manure they left the eggs of any flies behind. Because flies carry pinkeye from one animal to another, the lack of flies meant no infections. Bison had no need to develop a resistance to pinkeye.

In a pasture-based herd, the animals have no escape from the tormenting flies. As a result on our farm, pinkeye came to the herd in some degree every year. A vaccine is available against pinkeye, but I found it to be ineffective for our herd. In addition, it is short lived, you have to put the animal through the squeeze chute to inject it, and it must be done at a time of year the animals are not usually worked. The vaccine was not worth the trauma to the animals or to me.

Some years there is not much problem from pinkeye, other years it is devastating. One animal stands out above all the others in my memory, Little Annie. She was a week old when pinkeye infected both of her eyes. She could not see a thing and it was painful. We watched her and her mother closely to make sure Annie was cared for.

Pinkeye starts with a painful watering of the eye. They squint against the sun and their face below the eye soon is wet from the eye watering. As the disease progresses the eye turns white. As their body fights the infection and blood reaches the area to help fight the infection, the eye turns a bright red. When the infection has run its course, the eye usually has a small white scar, sometimes has a white film over it like a cataract, but too often the eye is blind or even bulging from the socket.

Little Annie was having trouble keeping up with her mother whose instinct to stay with the herd was strong. After about a week of trying to care for her blind daughter, her mom left her behind to join the herd. It was time for Leon and I to step in to help Annie.

Annie may have been blind, but she could still run when frightened – in circles and really fast. Poor babe! It was quite a rodeo for me to catch her. I finally caught a leg good enough to pull her to the ground and hold her. Annie was taken to the creep pen and fed a bottle of lambs milk replacer. She stopped fighting when her stomach was full. I had become Annie's mother and it would be a long road.

Luckily for Annie, she had been with her mother for that first week and had gotten her mother's first milk that gave her immunity. Except for her eyes, Annie was a very healthy little buffalo girl. My next priority was getting medicine from the veterinarian to doctor her eyes. We tried everything under the sun to treat her to no avail. Pinkeye is a virus and as you probably know, few viruses respond to antibiotics. I even tried mild salt solutions. Sometimes, like with the salt, there was a temporary improvement, then the infections set in again with a vengeance.

I was bottle feeding Annie twice a day and she had hay in the pen as well. It was so frustrating to be feeding her and looking at those infected eyes. One Saturday morning I headed to the farmers market after feeding Annie and my frustration must have kept Annie in the forefront of my mind. For some reason I told the story of Annie to a lady and her two sons at the market that morning. "Have you tried Ionic Silver in her eyes?" the lady asked. No, I had never heard of it. "We'll make you some and bring it out this afternoon." the lady said.

The three of them arrived that afternoon bearing a brown bottle full of WATER. Hummm. I'm not expecting miracles I told them. We went to Annie's pen – she was now in the pen next to the corral across the road where her mother lived outside and she could graze on fresh grass. As I gave Annie her bottle, we used an eye dropper to drop the silver water into her goopey eyes.

I was amazed the next morning when I went out to give Annie her bottle. Three quarters of the infected goop was gone from her eyes. Really? It was a miracle after everything that had been tried and I instantly became a believer in ionic silver solution. And to think it could be made at home! By Thursday all the goop was gone from her eyes. There was no more infection. Annie's eyes were blind as a bat from the damage done by the pinkeye virus. At least she was out of pain and healthy, and blind.

Annie was getting pretty big by now and insistent when it came to getting fed. Now that she was cured, I hoped to let her back with the herd. She could follow me by sound and scent and really hurt now if she stepped on my foot. She could follow the ATV too and was enjoying running with me. I led her back to the house to join the herd there where it would be easier for me to care for her. When I came into the pasture, she would run to me for her bottle, so feeding her was no problem.

It was sad to watch her play with the other buffalo babes. She would be running with joy then BONG right into a tree. All in all though, Annie seemed to be adapting and I no longer had to bottle feed her. Annie's story also has a sad ending. She got caught in the barb wire fence and by the time I found her, she was dead. I loved my beautiful blind buffalo daughter and it was a blessing to have her in my life. Even more, it was a blessing to have learned about ionic silver.

When Annie had responded so incredibly to the ionic silver solution, I instantly tried to learn all about it, including how to make it when this precious jar I had been given was gone. Making the silver solution turned out to be as simple as you could possibly imagine, once the little machine was made. Annie's angels who brought that jar also showed me the machine her father, a doctor, had made for her. But he had done such a good job housing the 'in-nerds' that I had not seen how it actually works.

What is needed to make the silver solution is distilled water, two silver coins or wires, and an ac adapter like you would plug your cell phone into the wall with, or maybe plug in power tools to charge the battery. Oh, and two alligator clips. You take the ac adapter and cut off the end that plugs into the phone or tool, then separate the two wires that are inside the cut wire. Strip the ends of the two wires and attach an alligator clip to each wire. Use the alligator clips to clip the two coins to the inside of a quart jar or similar container, then fill the container with distilled water making sure the alligator clips does not touch the water. Plug the adapter into the wall socket and leave plugged in for an hour.

The process of electrolysis is taking place in the jar, as the electricity flows from one coin to the other, positive to negative current. You don't have to worry about getting shocked as the ac adapters are typically only six volts. You probably won't even feel a thing if you stick your hand in the water, though I've never tried it. After about an hour, there will be roughly five parts per million silver in the water. That is not much. You won't see it or taste it, but that is what killed the virus in Annie's eyes.

The only words of caution I would give you is to be sure to use pure silver coins that say .9999 pure silver right on them, not silver clad or German silver or some other description as required by law. Also be sure to use distilled water. If other materials come in contact besides silver and water, you will end up with a compound when the silver combines with other substances. It will still be in solution and is called colloidal silver. Such a compound could well be poison, but the dose so minimal as to be unlikely to cause a problem – it just won't work as well as the ionic silver. A silver ion is smaller than an atom and unstable, wanting to attach to something and is small enough to kill a virus.

If you got too much silver in your body, it would not 'harm' you, but could turn your skin permanently a gray color. Ionic silver is not strong enough to do that even if you drank a gallon a day. Other compounds deliver a stronger dose of silver and excessive use has been known to turn people gray. EPA calls it a cosmetic problem. USDA refers to ionic silver as dangerous, but if you look deeper it is only because you may not get medical attention and there is no guarantee of how much silver is in the solution you just made.

If you go to a health food store, you can likely buy a **two** ounce bottle of Sovereign Silver for around twelve dollars. It is guaranteed to be ten parts per million of ionic silver. So **four** ounces of your homemade hour solution would deliver the same amount of ionic silver. My friends, that is over seven hundred dollars for a gallon of ionic silver that you could make for under a dollar at home.

My neighbor borrows my machine and makes about a gallon a month and uses it often. I only use it myself when I think I am coming down with a cold or have been exposed to some illness. I have rarely gotten any infection since I had access to treatment with ionic silver. And after around ten years of use, you can still read the writing on the coins. They will never be used up.

I was still so excited about Annie's miraculous recovery that I made up a flyer to tell people all about it and handed them out at the farmers market. One lady came back later that summer to tell me that her little boy had gotten pinkeye. She took him to the doctor who gave her a prescription and told her he would be fine in ten days. Instead of filling the prescription, she made a silver machine and put the silver in her son's eyes. He was fine in three days.

Before penicillin and other antibiotics were discovered, silver was one of the few medicines available to doctors and they came in many different compounds. Now doctors tends to look at modern medicine and not silver. But silver still is used. Countless babies eye sight has been saved over the years because silver nitrate in put in their eyes at birth to prevent blindness from gonorrhea. And silver is used with burns because it is effective and gentle to grievously burned patients. If you know folks who want to be prepared for long term disasters, tell them they should research ionic silver.

The Stockman Grassfarmer published another story that I wrote. It was called Annie's Angels and the Ionic Silver Machine. The response from farmers who's herds were 'organic' was the most common group to follow up with silver. Here on the farm, silver was to play an important roll in the future health of the buffalo.

Now that we have covered the pinkeye problem in depth, its time to move on to the next health issue, a disease called malignant catharral fever or MCF. This is a disease of sheep and for them it is like getting a cold and not considered a problem. Roughly eighty percent of sheep are carriers of the illness. It is an air born illness, just like a cold. If a bison comes into contact with a sheep when it is experiencing an active infection – like in spring or fall especially – it becomes fatal. Bison are what is called a 'dead end host' to MCF. They cannot spread it to other bison, but they will die. It is crucial that bison not be kept near flocks of sheep.

Most diseases of cattle can be spread to bison, not just pinkeye. As strong, hardy animals, they resist such illnesses, but may succumb to them. The disease you likely hear about the most is brucellosis. This is kind of like a ruminant venereal disease and causes the animals to abort calves.

The US government has done a good job of eradicating this disease in private herds by requiring any diseased animal to be destroyed. Public herds are now the source of the disease, principally in the bison and elk in the Yellowstone area. Ranchers are concerned that animals leaving the park could infect their private herds and the economic effect on their ranches would be devastating. The government has been unable to control the disease in the public herd and brucellosis remains an issue in the surrounding states.

For bison, the most serious health issue is intestinal parasites. Like flies, intestinal parasites are something free-ranging bison would have left behind. Eggs of the parasite are deposited in the manure, hatch, and the larvae crawl up on grasses to be consumed by the herd pastured there. In nature, the bison would be long gone before those larvae hatched out. Bison did not develop any immunity to intestinal parasites and an infestation is debilitating if not deadly to the buffalo.

A number of 'wormer' medications have been developed to control intestinal parasites in domestic animals. They can be injected, poured on, given in feed or in water and provide excellent control when delivered in a timely manner. As with antibiotics, parasites are developing an immunity to wormers. When these wormers become unreliable, it will create serious conditions for farms, including and maybe especially bison farms.

While injections, pour on wormers, or oral drenches are the most effective for protecting bison, getting them wormed requires putting the whole herd through the working facilities to the squeeze chute. This is expensive and traumatic and can result in the death of wild animals like bison. Worming is usually done in Spring and Fall, with another worming added if animals start looking poorly at other times. If worming is not done, it is highly likely that animals will die from the infestation and any that survive will not thrive.

Ranchers who can afford large herds and the property to support them will likely have the necessary working facilities needed. On smaller properties, especially in more eastern states, the equipment if often out of the financial reach of most bison owners. Compromises and co-operative efforts help here, but still worming the bison can be a challenge.

I found myself at a crossroads. I was widowed and dealing with the emotional issues of losing a spouse after forty three years – but the buffalo needed me. They were going downhill, obviously in need of worming. I tried the easy ways, wormer in the water, safeguard blocks, ineffectively trying to spray the most in need. It wasn't working. The last straw came when herd bull Quannah died. The herd HAD to be wormed and I was not up to working the whole large herd through the equipment. I considered it a desperate measure when I took range cubes into the pen and doused them with the pour on wormer and loose minerals that contained higher amount of the mineral selenium. I let the herd into the pen and prayed.

They ate it! I still waited and prayed. Would they be harmed by eating the pour on? They were fine and as the days passed the herd looked better and better. They were going to be OK now. The veterinarian assured me that even though it was not a way that was approved on the label, you did what needed to be done. It would do from now on as well. The animals not only were not stressed by the worming, they thought this was a real treat. I could handle this.

This method of worming was like magic, but I finally ran into a problem with one young heifer. She was in need of worming, but did not come into the feeding area with the herd. She had a bulging eye due to pinkeye the year before and was really skittish.

My young friend Rowdy who had started a buffalo herd near by called to ask if I had wormed the herd yet. I told him I had gotten all but one. He offered to come over with his new dart rifle to worm her. He had wormed his herd that way. We rode around the herd trying to get a shot at Solo, but she was too wise. She could tell that we were watching her and kept the herd between us. We were never able to dart her.

I locked the herd into the pen with treats again and opened a gate into the corral for the new Solo who was by now emaciated. It was awhile before she came into the pen but I was patiently waiting for her. I locked her in that pen for three days with nothing to eat that did not have wormer on it. If she ever ate anything, I couldn't tell. I should run her through the squeeze chute and inject her with wormer, but I couldn't handle the equipment by myself. It was Easter weekend and there was no one around that I could call for help. Finally, I let her go thinking it was a death sentence for her but could not be helped.

To my surprise, Solo started to put on weight and was no longer skin and bones. Soon she was blooming and was bred that summer. She must have eaten some of the wormer after all. The following spring she had a gorgeous baby girl, as black as she was. I would not have to worry about worming the herd in the future, just do it in a timely manner and pray that resistance to the wormer did not develop. And on a positive note, because the herd was wormed, there was no buildup of parasites in the pasture to reinfect the herd. They all looked wonderful!

Over the years I have lost three cows in childbirth when they prolapsed, which means they pushed so long and hard that the uterus was pushed out of her body and she bled to death. We lost some calves in childbirth. They looked healthy and fine but never got up. There have been four sets of twins that we knew of but the mothers had difficulty keeping both and I'll settle for single births. Occasionally an animal died of unknown causes, we just found a carcass. Only one animal I know of was ever shot and it had gotten over onto a neighbor's property. You can't always choose your neighbors.

Most birthing problems have occurred in first calf heifers who, like Rosie, are not mature enough at three to calve easily. After a stormy night I went into the field to check on the herd and found Dorothy in labor. I watch closely so I can be there to witness the birth if possible. But baby did not come. For two days the baby did not come. I called Doc Wooten to get his advice. It sounds like birthing trauma he said. There is a baby somewhere. Well I looked for that baby without a lot of hope in finding the carcass. After two days, dogs or coyotes likely would have taken it off. I had no luck finding it.

As I was opening the gate to leave the pasture, my male Pyrenees dog was standing in the middle of the field barking at me, like Lassie, "come here, come here!" This was so unusual that I closed the gate and went to Murphy. He turned and led me to the back fence and there standing in the tall weeds was a baby buffalo. Oh, Wow!

I went back to the house and made up a bottle of lambs milk replacer. It was too late to worry about colostrum as the baby needs that within the first 12 hours. After that their stomach changes and they cannot absorb the large molecules. I headed back out to the field to the little one. I caught her reasonably easily but she was fighting like a buffalo against me and would not take the bottle. I needed to get Leon's help to get her in the car and back to the pen. As I was walking back to the ATV, I looked behind me and she was following me!

I was afraid that if I started the bike she would run away, so I walked all the way across the pasture with her behind me. When we got to the creep pen she took the bottle from me. I was now a buffalo mother again. I named her Tootsie after my friend Dorothy's nickname. She was buffalo Dorothy's babe after all. I did manage to get buffalo Dorothy in the pen with Tootsie for three days, but it did not help. There was no recognition, Dorothy wanted back with the herd and she was scaring the baby.

I was told if you put the baby's hair in the mother's food, she would take the baby. That had not worked either. I let Dorothy go and resigned to bottle feeding a babe again. Bottle feeding is a big commitment. You are tied to that baby for months and she would not take the bottle from anyone but me.

What a joy that babe was to me. She followed me everywhere I went, so each day we would go into the pasture to be with the herd. When she was left there, she would stay until I came back to feed her again. At night I left her in the creep pen. After about a week, Tootsie began lagging behind the herd as they went on to graze. Then I noticed that she was having painful urination as bladder infection had set in. Oh, no..... I remembered sweet Holly and how the fight against infection had been useless. But I had a new medicine in the arsenal now, ionic silver.

From that day on, a fresh batch of ionic silver was made twice a day and used to make Tootsie's lamb's milk. She was weak and listless now and I moved her into the hay barn where she had a nice nest to lay in. Murphy and Smurphy, the two Great Pyrenees dogs kept her company and guarded her. When Tootsie finished her bottle, we would sit in the grass and I would pick tender leaves of grass and clover to stuff into the side of her mouth. She would have refused it if I had let her, but she needed bulk in her diet.

As I sat with Tootsie and petted her I would sing lullabys to her, "There's an island out in the seas where the babies all grow on trees", "Great big dog come down the meadow and shock his tail and shock the meadow" and so on. You'd be really feeling sorry for Tootsie right now if you could hear me sing...

Tootsie was not getting any better, but then she was not getting worse either. As the days grew longer and hotter, Tootsie was moved into the shade of the back yard with the dogs and rooster to keep her company. She was so weak, I wondered if maybe something, possibly even the silver, might be limiting the amount of selenium she was getting, causing white muscle disease. My friends Mike and Janie had lost two healthy calves to a selenium deficiency caused by too much protein in the mother's diet.

At the feed store, I was told that selenium injections had to be prescribed by a veterinarian and that there was one a few blocks away. At that office I explained the situation to a veterinarian I had never met. He told me to 'stop giving her that stuff', meaning the silver, gave me a selenium syringe and told me if that didn't work, we should give Tootsie a 'real antibiotic'. I gave Tootsie the shot, but nothing changed. And I didn't use the silver that evening or the following morning in Tootsie's milk. By afternoon her little knees were swollen like grapefruits. She got silver that evening in her milk and continued to get it after that.

I went back to the same veterinarian on Monday to discuss the 'real antibiotic' he would recommend. He asked if I was still giving Tootsie 'that stuff' and I told him what happened, but that if he could give me an antibiotic I could put in her milk, I was certainly willing to give that a try. So she got the 'real antibiotic' for ten days with no change.

It was impossible for me to go anywhere without taking Tootsie along if I was gone over half a day. So Tootsie went to the Missouri Bison Association meeting near Springfield for an overnight stay. We made a pen in the yard for her, but she was uncomfortable in the strange environment and ended up spending the night in the van. She also made an all day drive with me across the state to Hannibal, Missouri for a family reunion. This time she stayed in her little

pen with the market umbrella over her for the week, then did fine on the return trip home. I had a rope halter for her to lead her around, but it was not necessary. She was not going to leave me even if she got spooked. I was her mother.

Tootsie was about three months old before her natural immunity kicked in. Finally her energy was back and she was playing in the yard with the dogs. When visitor came to

the farm, the dogs would come running to greet them and here came Tootsie right behind them. But she was shy and never let anyone else pet her except me and my own mother. When it was time for her milk, I would go sit on the ATV near the front door and call her. I didn't have to go find her, she always came running. Her favorite sleeping spot was now the front porch. If I took the ATV across the road to visit the other herd, Tootsie ran along behind me. Often the herd over there would chase her and I would have to go retrieve her when she ran away from them.

Tootsie thanks my mom for a drink of water while traveling to the family reunion in the van.

The dogs often went into the pasture and Tootsie went too. She had a number of secret passages into the field, like going through our wood shop's open back door, past the hay barn and out the creep entrance of the creep pen. Unfortunately she also played on the road at night with the dogs and the neighbors let me know. They could see the white dogs on the road, but not Tootsie and she was liable to get hit.

It was time for Tootsie to live in the pasture and be a buffalo. That also meant finding all her secret passages into and out of the field. It didn't take her long to learn it was really fun being a buffalo. And the dogs were probably relieved that she was gone by then. Its natural for buffalo to have a pecking order and she was now considerably bigger than the 150 pound dogs and had become their boss.

Tootsie had not been getting a bottle for months now. Lamb's milk replacer was expensive and she was doing just fine without it. But I was still her mother and she came running any time I went into the pasture. I would have to go through the gate farthermost from her, or she would get there before I could get the gate closed. If she stepped on my feet in her eagerness to see me, it really hurt. So Tootsie would meet the ATV half way and run with me with joy. It was just like she was before the infections had set in.

All was well until Tootsie was three years old. Suddenly she was in the front yard every day that winter. How was she getting out? If Tootsie could get out, the rest of the herd could too. It snowed and I tried following her tracks to see her secret entrance, but I guess I'm no tracker. I still could not find out how she was getting in the yard. Finally I spotted her get out. There was now a hole in the back of that hundred year old barn and the side door out front was open where Little Wonder had gone in to hide. All I had to do was shut that front door and Tootsie could no longer escape. A fence has since been put across the back of the barn to help protect it. I'm hoping with care, that barn might last another hundred years.

While buffalo typically have their first calf when they are three, Tootsie did not have a calf that year. I was concerned that maybe she had developed poorly and would never be a mother. Then one day that summer when Tootsie came running to meet me, Gorgeous George was running with her. She was being courted and Gorgeous was not about to let her get away from him. I tried to get away from Tootsie to no avail. This was her favorite game and George was keeping in step. I hit a rock and thought "This is not good. How am I going to get away? I can't get back out the gate without them catching up with me." Shades of Lolita, I went to park by some of the older girls. Tootsie was not allowed to be in their circle and had to stop about twenty feet away. So I sat with the other girls and watched Tootsie be courted.

On the fourth spring, I became a grandmother to Tootsie's daughter Caroline. She has since become a mother many times. Finally there was a way to save buffalo children from infections using the ionic silver. Tootsie has her own page over at my website, *www.ourbuffalofarm.com*.

Chapter 17   The Drought

I spend much of my time with the buffalo. They don't talk much, but they say a lot. Their body language speaks volumes and their eyes are amazing! There is a depth to them that makes me think they know far more about life and the world than I can ever comprehend. When I look into those eyes, it makes me try to understand as a buffalo would. I hope you will enjoy the view "through buffalo eyes".

The Drought

There was a hint of amusement and surprise shinning
from deep pools of understanding
in the eyes of the buffalo.
Those eyes spoke eloquently.
"You feel sorry for us?
Yes, its true that there is drought across much of the country,
and many buffalo will face the hardships of winter
on half-empty stomachs.....
But that is not new to us. This is our country.
We were born here in the days when no humans looked after us.
That's why we have these warm winter coats and slow our metabolism
when the days grow short.
If you want to feel sorry for someone,
then look over the fence
at the cattle and horses."
"We may not all survive. Its always been that way.
But those who do survive will have grown stronger.
We know that Spring will come and the grass will green.
There will be calves to give new life to the earth and restore our herds.
You will see.
The legacy of the buffalo will live and grow."

Nature is so beautiful, we forget how harsh it can be at times. When buffalo roamed free across the land, prairie fires were cruel in their path. Swollen rivers had currents that even the strongest bison could not overcome. River banks would become littered with their carcasses for miles down stream. Blizzards and deep snow hid food sources for months on end. Yet the bison endured.

People ask me if fireworks and gunshots scare my herd. I have to smile. Have you ever been out in a thunder storm? Flashes of lightening lighting up the sky and thunder rolling right through you? Rain heavy enough to drown you? That is the bison's world. When blizzards came storming in, the bison turned to face the storm and walked right on through it. Contrast that to cattle who drifted with the wind and stayed longer in the path of the storm.

Deep snows were left in the wake of the blizzards and cattle look around for the hay pile. Bison used their big heads and strong necks to move the snow away from the grass below. The large hump over the shoulder provided an anchor for those strong neck muscles to leverage from.

Some years Yellowstone provides a window to winters that even the hardy bison cannot survive. An early snow begins to melt, then freezes to a hard thick layer of ice. The grass below is no longer accessible. In years like that, as many as two thirds of the bison do not survive. In a no win spiral, bison stand in the hot waters when temperatures drop many degrees below freezing. There is no food in the hot spring. At the sub-zero temperatures they need to starting burning body fat to stay warm, but there is very little body fat left to sustain them. If I allowed my herd to suffer that way, I would be charged with animal cruelty.

The survivors of those winter conditions are the strongest, best fed of the herd. But while their body frames are emaciated, when food is once again available they fill out quickly to the beautiful animals that went into winter. The cycle of birth begins again.

These magnificent animals in my pasture were honed by centuries of surviving through the beauty and horror of nature. They have not been domesticated by man. No, they are wild animals still. Open the gate and they will take off on their own to do what bison do naturally – roam and eat. If you want a closer look at bison in nature and history, I would recommend you find The Buffalo Book by David Dary. Its one of the best written books you could ask for. And you will learn why bison can no longer roam wild and free.

I feel blessed each time that I enter the buffalo's herd and am allowed to be a part of it. They are very quiet, but their body language allows excellent communication between us. And I do always talk to them with my voice, even though they don't answer me. They watch my mouth and face and hear the sound of my voice and know I am with them and they do not need to fear me. It is always a pleasure when any bison comes to me on their own. I understand that some of the draw is the ATV that they love to rub on – but they think that is me as well.

When we returned Prince George to his father's herd as a thousand pound two year old, he bellowed the news of his return to his rightful place as future monarch of the herd. Gorgeous George proudly wrestled with his son every day, teaching everything he needed to know. The bouts were not serious, but Prince gave them his all to impress this massive father. Prince would not be fully mature until he was seven, so he had a long way to go yet.

As the years passed, it was inevitable that one day there would be the very serious fight between father and son to establish who would be in charge of breeding the beautiful cows. I did not get to witness the fight, but Prince got the honors that summer. Gorgeous George stayed back to appraise the job his son was doing, but you could tell he was thinking "Enjoy it while you can. I'm just taking a break this year. Think I'll take the job back next year."

I missed the brawl the next year as well, but Gorgeous George bred the ladies that year while Prince stood back with obvious irritation. It just was not fair. Next year Prince intended to show his father who was in charge. They were really well matched at that point in time.

Teach his father Prince did the next summer. He must have really been holding a grudge. Not only defeated, Gorgeous George was banned from the herd entirely. I would look out the window and see Prince stalking along behind his father relentlessly, keeping him totally away from the herd. It was sad to watch. George had done such a wonderful job as herd bull from the time he arrived at our farm and had produced beautiful buffalo children for us. Now there was no longer room for him. His job was done and he no longer had a home.

There was a LOT of meat on Gorgeous George and processing him instead of letting him be miserable just made sense. It was with sadness but appreciation that George was sent to Clouds for his final ride. The meat would be too tough for steaks and roasts, but the flavor would have gotten better with age. The meat would all be burger. It was mixed with a meat of a culled cow to give it at least a little fat content, the mix being about ninety seven percent lean. We had thought that someday we would mount George's head, but we just could not.

Prince had fine genetics and had learned well from his father. We knew we had made the right decision to keep him as herd bull. Because he was born at our farm, he was familiar with us and I felt safer with Prince than I had with George.

We did have one run in though that I for one will NEVER forget. It was a beautiful Spring day and I drove the ATV into the field to check on the progress of calving in the herd. They were laying in the woods at the far back of the pasture. I didn't have to worry about them getting out, so I left the gate open behind me – mistake, big time. I sat with the herd for awhile, still one of my greatest pleasures, until I saw Prince get up and start grazing across the field. Nothing exciting was happening so I might as well go back to the house.

Turns out that Prince was not just 'accidentally' grazing in the direction of the open gate. He wanted to investigate the possibilities. When I came out of the woods, Prince started running toward the gate. I gave it the gas and was soon racing him. Prince took exception to my actions and turned to run after me! I was going full speed and turned at the east fence then turned again when I neared the front woods, with Prince thundering ten feet behind me. Now the open gate was in front of me and I figured that if he had not caught me by now, he was not going to. But what would happen when I went through that gate?!

Though the gate I went, put on breaks and looked behind me. Prince had stopped the other side of the gate and was rolling in the dirt. I shut that gate as fast as I could and never leave it open after that no matter where the herd might be. I could just see Prince saying to himself, "I guess I showed her whose pasture this is!" Yeah, he definitely chased me out that time.

Here in the Ozarks, weather is typically mild. But sometimes it throws a tantrum and does things like drop ten inches of rain just to make it flood, or gets super cold and snows to mess up the roads. Ice is usually more of a problem than snow here. And there can be a devastating tornado such as the one in Joplin that killed hundreds of folks. One year an ice storm brought down trees and power line so much that we were without power for ten days. The electric company is a co-operative owned by the users and tries to do a great job of keeping the lines clear and refunds some of our electric bill to us if it there is left over money at the end of the year.

I think the drought is the worse weather event of them all. It is drawn out over such a long period of time that it wears you down. First you think its getting pretty dry out there. Then its real dry and we need some rain. The grass and clover are withering in the fields. We need rain bad again. But it doesn't rain and the grass is dry and you don't see how it could ever grow again. But you know it will, if it just would rain. Its depressing to watch at the pasture turns to dirt and dust. Now when the bison roll in their wallows, great clouds of dust blow in the air.

We're losing topsoil now every time the wind blows. Still the rains don't come. Statistics show that farmers have a high suicide rate. I expect that if you were to co-relate suicide to weather events, you would find one of the main causes. Everything you work for and dream is going up in dust and you are helpless to do anything about it.

That is what it was like here one summer. We were declared a disaster area and could expect federal assistance to recover. But financial assistance does not come until many months or even a year later. And financial assistance does not make it rain. Ponds were drying up. Thank goodness we have the rural water district, out animals will have plenty to drink. For people not so lucky in their area, the volunteer fire department was using their tanker truck to haul water to livestock in need. Depression turned to hopelessness as the drought dragged on into fall.

We had to start feeding hay to the herd in June that year. We should have still been cutting hay, instead we were feeding it. What they were eating was their winter's supply of food and that was going to be a real problem down the road. Bison's metabolism slows in the winter and they don't need as much hay as cattle. In the summer though, they have healthy appetites and need plenty to eat. In past drought, ragweed had been an important food source even though they normally didn't eat it. This year even the ragweed was gone.

In winter, bison fill their stomachs with hay, then go out to 'recreational graze' in the short grass left in the winter pasture. Here during the drought there was nothing green in the fields except prickly thistles. Thistles are such a nuisance that the law requires farmers to control it. The pretty prickly blossoms turn to a fluff like dandelions and blow for miles onto other property as well as where they were growing. I was shocked to see the bison eating those flowers. Surely it would damage their mouth! I watched as Mariah parked herself in a thistle patch and proceeded to feast on the blossoms all around her.

I had started mowing the thistles, I was supposed to control them. But the bison were following along behind the tractor using their tongues to lick up the white fluff that had fallen from the flowers. Wow. They were eating so much thistle that I estimated it provided possibly ten percent of their diet. Lets see, they were eating a bale of hay a day, those big round bales that weigh nearly a ton. Ten percent would be about three bales a month. Bales were expensive this year, around forty five dollars each. That is over a hundred dollars a month the thistles would save in food. And the animals liked the variety it provided in their diet and it satisfied their instinct to graze. Suddenly thistles were no longer a 'weed'. My definition of a weed was something the buffalo did not eat. Others might define a weed differently, but this was my farm.

Depression cannot be avoided under these circumstances and I was not immune. One thing that really irritated me was Prince and his big assistant. All they did was lay around in the hay bales all day and eat their bed. I was thinking they were eating more than the rest of the herd combined. And hay was running out! What happens then?

It was desperate times on the farm. I called a livestock broker. Was he interested in a couple of mature bison bulls. They are always in demand for hunting preserves or bison burger. They were interested. It was impressive to watch them sort the two big bulls from the herd and then load them into the trailer. Trust me, it was not that simple. Getting them in the pen is fairly easy, as the bulls are the dominant animals in the herd and are first in line when there is food available. But letting them in the pen where you are is a dangerous proposition.

The men's only complaint was that my herd was hard to handle because they were not afraid of people and could not be pressured easily by human presence. I could not have accomplished what these experts did that day. When the two animals were safely aboard their trailer, they handed me a check for a very reasonable amount. It would buy the hay for winter IF I COULD FIND IT.

And so we said goodbye to Prince George. He was a good boy, but there were a couple of his sons in the herd who would be just fine to step up and carry on his legacy. The rains still had not come and hay had to be found. The herd may have to be fed through fall as well as winter.

Let me step away for a bit and give you an idea of what the drought was like during the dust bowl days in the 1930s. Here are a couple of exerts from the local paper in 1934.

"The best of the dairy cattle purchased by the government in drouth areas are going to be distributed to families on the relief rolls and in need of good dairy cows."

"Farmers in the 20 drought stricken states have received a total of more than $32,000,000 in payment for cattle purchased by the agricultural adjustment administration."

"The McDonald County relief organization is now being called upon to aid 1,300 families representing approximately 6,000 people, which is nearly one-half the population of the county."

"The drouth has made it necessary for many who have always made a living by farming to ask for help. All the applicants ask for is a chance."

Yeah, droughts get my vote as the worst of the natural disasters. Nothing lives without water. The search was on to find hay for our herd. The neighbors with a dairy took out bank loans to buy hay from Mississippi for $40 per bale but had to add another $40 a bale to have it shipped here. And dairy cows eat a lot all winter, unlike bison.

We turned to our hay supplier friend. He had not cut much hay that year and it was all sold. But he located some for us for $35 per bale plus $5 to haul it for us. What a relief! But you would not have believed that hay could have so much trash in it!. It must have been baled along a highway and anything that could be thrown or blown out of a vehicle had been baled up with the hay. Soon our pasture would look like it was next to a freeway. By October the rains finally came.

Just writing this story of the drought brings back fears of what summer could be like again. We have a hay barn now and can stockpile hay when it is plentiful. That would help get through bad times weather wise, but the psychological effects likely would still be devastating.

Thistle still grows in the pastures, getting rid of it is pretty much near impossible and its good that the bison still help some in controlling them. Seems that especially the bulls still enjoy biting off those blossoms. It may be a weed, but I don't describe it a a noxious weed any longer.

The plains states have few trees, as between wild fires and bison trees didn't have a chance. Here in the Ozarks, trees are the norm, not pastures, field crops or prairie. The woods are full of oak, walnut, hickory, persimmon, sassafras and numerous other species of trees. If pastures are not mowed at LEAST once a year, trees begin to take over again. We usually call the mowing 'brush hogging', Its not only the trees, but brambles of all kinds especially blackberries and multiflora rose. Yes, wild roses.

There are wonderful flowering trees in the spring, redbud and dogwood being the favorite. Its amazing to watch in spring as the world turns from drab to brilliant greens with flowers everywhere. The oak trees are leafless for six months of the year, but are a fine food source for animals in the woods. Its the same for many other trees as well. I enjoy the woods as much as the pastures.

We have finished fencing the pastures across the road with electric fences and moved the second herd to their new home. It is so much easier now to care for the herd, mow fields, put out hay an so on. It is incredibly beautiful property with rocky bluffs and many springs and ponds.

The only nasty I have not been able to control is a weed called cockleburr. Each fall the burrs get in the bison's wool like Velcro and just make a mess. And unlike thistle, it is totally inedible. Mowing sets it back for a few weeks, then its back again. Spraying will kill it, but in the process kill the clovers as well. Ideally to kill cockleburr, we should spray it a couple of years then reseed the clover. It is doubtful that would ever eradicate the problem as the land is to rough to get into all the areas and any weed left behind would start it all over again. At least that's been my number one excuse not to spray.

Fall in the Ozarks comes close to rivaling Spring with its beauty. The cool season grasses grow with abandon and no seed heads are there to get in the way of the grazing animals. The bison sock on the weight to be in shape for winter. We as ranchers need to make sure the herd gets wormed again in fall so they can thrive.

Winter is a time for the world to rest on its glory. We typically don't get much snow, more likely ice storms. When snow does come, we can just enjoy it while its here because it will be gone in a day or two. The trees now being bare of leaves allows us to see many things otherwise hidden in a blanket of green. The limestone bluffs are one such feature. We even see houses that have been hidden, river courses, rocks in the field that break equipment when hidden by the greenery. On sunny windless days, being outside on a winter day is even more delightful than a summer day and I spend such days with my buffalo family.

Nature's beauties fill the heart with joy. Maybe we need the disasters to remind us just how wonderful life really is.

Chapter 18 They Know We are Here

As the crow flies, Oakcreek Buffalo Ranch is a mile from the Arkansas/Missouri state line. That is also the Mason Dixon Line and the area is as rich in history as it is in natural beauty. South of the line, less than twenty miles away is the corporate headquarters of probably the largest company in the country, Walmart. Its presence has caused the area to grow wildly in the years since we moved to the farm and it is now considered the Northwest Arkansas Major Metropolitan Area. Even our rural county with less than thirty thousand population is a part of that.

Bordering McDonald County to the north of us is the Joplin Major Metropolitan Area. We are an island of beauty and peacefulness that attracts folks who want to escape the city. On Summer weekends, tens of thousands of 'tourists' flock to our waterways such as Elk River, Sugar Creek and Indian Creek for floating and camping. To get to Oakcreek Buffalo Ranch, you cross a nice new bridge over Little Sugar Creek and find yourself in rural farmland that looks much the same as it did a hundred years ago. Leon always said turning down our Hollow was like going through Alice's looking glass. Each day the view changes with the seasons and the weather and satisfies the soul.

Less than twenty miles to the west is the Oklahoma State Line. A hundred years ago it was known as Indian Territory. Our county was the jumping off area for government and other trappings of 'civilization'. It was a wild area with plenty of history especially during the civil war. Our courthouse was burned down by Jayhawkers and rebuilt shortly after the war. That courthouse now houses the most wonderful museum showcasing the county's history! Oakcreek Buffalo Ranch proudly became the first sponsor of a room in a museum that has far exceeded anyone's expectations.

In 1939, the wonderfully classic Jesse James movie was filmed in our county seat where the courthouse is, Pineville. Many of the scenes were filmed right in that building. Oakcreek's room is the Jesse James room and much memorabilia from the film is there, like the printing press used in the movie. Each August has Jesse James Day with a parade, amusement rides, and booths of all kinds.

Another fun event that gets it own room in the museum is the Succession. Back in the early 1960's when I was still in high school in Florida, McDonald County succeeded from the state of Missouri in a tiff because we were left off the state's tourism map. Tourism is the second largest source of income for the county behind only agriculture, and the tourism map was very important. The area became McDonald Territory. There was a three hundred man militia organized, a land rush, stamps to get a letter posted to be sent to the US Mail, a land rush, and many other staged events.

Tribes offered to take McDonald County as a part of Indian Territory. Arkansas offered to annex the county to offset the boothill in the east. Joplin opened an embassy and Carthage sent down troops to try to 'force us back into Missouri'. The militia stopped every car, train, and bus that crossed the county line and issued 'visas' to the occupants. It was a fun time and was a wonderful stunt to generate publicity for the county. It was a pretty serious thing to do though and made lots of residents of the county nervous about things like social security and such. The succession was soon over.

I love this county and the folks here and proudly call it home for the rest of my life. When a fundraiser promised a community college a mile over the hill from the farm, Oakcreek made a serious endowment to the college even though it required a loan to manage. They were going to name the conference center Klein but I refused. They had to call it the Buffalo Room as the buffalo were going to have to pay for it. Its a pleasure to drive by the campus as I head to the new Walmart nearby. Now I'm spoiled to only have to drive five minutes to do my grocery shopping.

When Leon and I made the decision to raise buffalo, we had no idea it would create such a stir in the community. Sure, we could understand the neighbor's concerns as they would be directly affected by the animals nearby. The interest in the buffalo by the general public took us totally by surprise. After all, we had been inspired by a buffalo herd only about forty miles away, so it was not like there were no buffalo around. And later we found many buffalo even closer. We hired neighbors to reinforce the fences and they had done a great job, I guess in self defense. We understood that they were concerned with our lack of experience and were determined to learn and do the job right.

Within the first month of the buffalo girl's arrival, Leon and I attended a grazing school in Joplin put on by the Extension Service. While there we became acquainted with the agricultural reporter for the Joplin Globe, Mike Surbrugg. Mike came out to see the girls and do a story about them.

We had a small flat bed trailer that we hauled lumber into the shop with, and pulled that trailer with a ride on lawnmower. We used this to take the reporter out into the field with the babes, Mike and I ridding on the trailer and Leon driving the lawnmower. The girls surrounded us and begged for treats. Mike was smitten by the babes and wrote a wonderful story about them. A week later, we had visitors to the farm who had read the article and was interested in raising buffalo too. Would we introduce them to our herd? It was a pleasure of course to do just that.

One snowy winter day, Mike called and said it was a slow news day at the paper and he was wondering how the buffalo were enjoying the snow. They are loving it, I told him. Right now they are out in front of the house playing on the ice over the pond. Would he like pictures? That would be great. So I emailed pictures of the girls having their skating party on the pond. Mike returned to the farm each year to follow the progress of the herd and do another story. These stories had a wide readership and word was getting around about our buffalo herd.

The local paper does stories every few years about the herd over the years and ran pictures when twin babes were born. Then the Arkansas papers picked up the story and ran with it. There was even a television clip run from the farm by the Fayetteville, AR station. Next our story was picked up by wider read papers. At a conference field day for the bison association, the farm story was picked up by a larger national paper and so the herd became known really far and wide. We were enjoying sharing our story with the world.

Locally we have become well known simply by word of mouth. Folks love to come to the farm to buy meat and see the animals. They tell their friends and bring their visitors out for an outing they won't forget.

The website that started off with a buffalo trade had become mine to maintain. It was never turned over to professionals to promote, but I must have done something right. Currently it has had more than 109,000 visitors with around 180 visitors every day. I've added lots to it over the years, but have not updated it as much as I should.

I've been having much more fun with Facebook. Since my Facebook page https://www.facebook.com/carol.klein.988 does not get as many visitors as the website, I have a link to on the homepage to Facebook. Its so easy to post tons of pictures and videos there of the buffalo! Let me share a Facebook post from earlier this year.

2017 Started off with a potential disaster when Awesome was discovered with a broken leg on Monday, the day after Christmas. I have been taking food and water to him and have locked the herd out of the pasture he is in. This is him on this evening Thursday eating the grass I have been gathering for him. That has been difficult to find, so tomorrow will start him on hay.

I had a bit of an accident yesterday when hauling water to him. I was balanced on a tree root out in the pond to fill the bucket and when I turned with the heavy bucket, I lost my balance and fell into the pond. Completely dunked..... As I sat there thinking this is a fine mess - maybe I should take a selfie, I realized that my new cell phone was in my pocket under water. Oh no!

Suddenly it was not so funny. The phone was DOA, so today I have a new phone - same old number.

Life happens on the buffalo farm. And sometimes shit happens. I love it though and would not have it any other way.

Folks were rooting for Awesome from as far away as Alaska and Canada, and Georgia and Texas. You will be happy to know that Awesome recovered from his injuries and is back with the herd, happily courting the ladies. He still has a bit of a limp, but since it was a front foot that was injured, it should not affect his ability to breed.

Pretty Feather is welcoming Awesome back while the younger members of the herd look on.

Chapter 19   Visitors to the farm

The most interesting thing to me about the people who visit the farm is that you never know who will show up next. Sometimes it is a long time customer who has become a friend. Sometimes it is a new meat customer who has never seen buffalo up close. It may be people from other countries. They come from all over the world, European countries, Cuba, Russia, Africa, the list goes on and on. To bad I have not kept a world map to stick pens in for each visitor.

Sometimes people want to pay me for the 'tour' of the farm, that usually consists of taking range cubes to the creep pen and call the herd to us. When the buffalo see people in the pen, they know there will be treats. Calling them is just to get their attention to make sure they know they have visitors. When they come running there are exciting cheers from the folks who have come to see them. The buffalo ALWAYS get treats when I call them, so that they will come the next time.

When the buffalo arrive at the creep pen, the visitors throw range cubes out to the animals. If they want to feed them by hand, I warn them that they will have to be brave, and not jerk their hand back when the buffalo's long tongue reaches out to pull the food into their mouth. That would be like teasing them: "You want this? No, you can't have it." They usually have to be reminded that the buffalo cannot reach through the bars to get the food. After a few dropped cubes, most visitors manage to hand the cubes to the buffalo and are proud to have done so.

There are rules in the creep pen, like don't stick your arm out. The buffalo defend themselves – and reprimand people – usually by hitting them with a horn. So far no one has been hurt visiting the buffalo. I tell them the buffalo don't like to be petted like a dog. Your hand over their head is a threat. A hand below the head gets sniffed or licked as the buffalo satisfy their curiosity about their guests. Dogs have to be on a leash and controlled or they are likely to upset the buffalo or go through the fence to chase the buffalo and end up getting chased themselves. Most of the time, folks choose to leave their pets in their vehicle.

People want to 'feel' the buffalo and that can lead to problems. I have collected wool and a tanned hide in the meat room for people to feel and even a horn and skull. Its a surprise at first to learn that the horn is hollow, then they remember powder horns were made from buffalo and cattle horns. The horns are not like antlers, if they get knocked off, they do not grow back. I explain that I can tell the age and sex of a buffalo by their horns, the more curve, the older the animal. The biggest around belong to a bull. Looking at the horns is the first thing when trying to identify a buffalo in the herd.

I explain that the hump is an extension of the backbone to help anchor the strong neck muscles to hold up their massive heads. They are far stronger than a cow, run fast as a horse, are outstanding kickers, and can jump a fence from a standstill like a mule. When people try to pay me for the visit, I laugh and say I enjoy it so much, I might have to pay them. Sure I could charge for tours but I prefer to make friends for me and for the buffalo.

Guests encouraged me to tell all this in the book about the buffalo because it is interesting stuff that they had never known. So I decided I would share this story I wrote for the Missouri Bison Association cookbook to tell people about buffalo on the farm. I thought you might enjoy it here.

Buffalo Today

The newborn buffalo struggled to stand on wobbly legs, then flopped back down. His mother grunted encouragement and gave him a few happy licks with her long tongue. Once again he made a mighty effort and stood swaying. He had a great inward urge to find his mother's udder, where ever and what ever that was. After minutes of exploring his mother's underside, his search ended. The happy wagging of his tail told the world that this was worth the effort.

Members of the herd came to check out the new arrival, then went on with their eating. Curious calves gathered nearby. The new babe was fascinated with these little beings who were just his size and who seemed so friendly. When his woolly coat dried off, it would fluff up like theirs, and be the same soft pumpkin color. Soon he would be spending as much time with them as he did with his mother, playing, exploring and tasting everything in sight.

The days of summer grew longer, and then shorter again. The hair along the calves' back and around their eyes turned brown. Before long they lose all the orange baby color, and take on the buffalo brown of their mothers. Horns are now an inch long on the little bulls, and while visible are more delicate on the heifer babes. The herd bull is now courting the mother cows in their rutting season, making babes for the following spring.

With the coming of fall, the adult bison begin to grow a winter coat to protect them from the cold. They look like they are covered in velvet, then gradually a thick, woolly fur covers their bodies. The whole herd loves the crisp, cool days of fall. They thunder across the pastures in a full run or a bonging hop, for the joy of being alive and being buffalo. The calves now have a distinct hump. This bony protrusion from the backbone above the shoulders is an anchor for their strong neck muscles, enabling them to plow away snow for winter grazing. Winter cold will be pleasant for them, rather than a hardship. Their bodies adapt to the season by lowering their metabolism. They will not eat as much during winter and will grow little until spring.

Soon it will be time for the calves to be removed from their mothers. Most farms are small, and cannot keep these additional animals in their herds. Many of the babes are already spoken for, contracted by other farmers to expand herds or form new herds. The remainder will be taken to auction, or pastured together until sold or taken for meat.

As spring comes once more to the farm, the babes have become yearlings. Their horns and legs are growing longer and they take on the awkward, charming look of adolescents. It is a happy, carefree year for these young buffalo. Their job is to eat and grow, and enjoy life. They are very sociable animals, staying in a group virtually all the time. Yet they have developed strong individual personalities and a "pecking order" within the herd.

By the time these young bison reach their second birthday, they have matured into breeding age buffalo. Depending on their sex and genetics, they now weigh between 700 and 1,000 pounds. They will not reach their full size and maturity until they are seven years old when they can double their two year old weights. The two year old heifers will be placed in a breeding herd, as they will join in the rut this summer. Only the very biggest and best of the two year old bulls will join a breeding herd. These buffalo can live to twenty and even thirty or more years of age.

Buffalo cows in good condition will calve every twelve months, and twenty calves is not unreasonable to expect from these mothers. If bulls are not placed in the breeding herd, they will become meat animals before their third birthday. This young age will help insure the tenderness of the meat. Farms differ on how they feed these bulls to prepare them for slaughter. On some farms, they remain in the breeding herd, feeding on grass, until they are required for meat. Other producers prefer to finish the bulls on grain for a few months to maintain a control over the taste of meat as grass differs according to season, pasture, and weather. These animals will be separated into a meat herd and fed grain on pasture, or placed in confinement to be fed.

Although life is shorter for these bulls, it has been good. And their meat is not wasted, rather it provides nourishment so that humans can live and be healthy. This meat provides the necessary financial support for their herd and farm home to prosper.

When buffalo roamed these lands, wild and free, they adapted to their environment and multiplied into the millions of animals. Nature was not always kind. Blizzards, range wild fires, and droughts made life very difficult at times for the buffalo. The strongest animals survived, bred, and continued to multiply. It is no longer possible for buffalo to roam freely across this country. Farmers and ranchers, who admire the buffalo and chose to raise them, take on the responsibility of seeing that fenced herds are well fed, healthy, happy and safe. It is also their job to choose which animals will survive, breed and multiply.

Raising buffalo is a challenging and very rewarding job. It requires planning, understanding, and a lot of patience rather than strength and physical work. A buffalo is well fed when he is grazing on properly managed grass pastures. Grass hay is substituted when the pastures are dormant. The farmer must make sure that there are no more animals than the land can sustain. This can be challenging, as weather differs from year to year. Keeping the grass from over maturing or being over-grazed requires flexibility and close watch over the fields. If this job is well done by the farmer, the buffalo will enjoy a longer season on good grass and will require less expense for hay.

A well fed buffalo is a happy buffalo, if he also has the company of a herd. They do not like to be alone. This can make it difficult to sort animals from the herd when necessary to do so. They always want to stay together, and even more so when they feel threatened. Traditional protection for the buffalo has always been safety in numbers. Stronger animals will protect the herd from danger. These animals can out run horses, jump, kick, and use their horns very expertly. If the buffalo are not happy, they will be very difficult to keep in any pasture. The farmer definitely wants his buffalo to be very happy.

A well fed, happy buffalo is a very strong, healthy animal. There are diseases which can spread from neighboring beef herds to the bison. Because of the sturdiness of the bison this rarely happens. But most farmers will vaccinate at least the calf herd against bovine disease as a precaution against the stress of weaning. Whether or not the animals are vaccinated, the farmer keeps close watch on the physical condition of his herd, watching for any signs of poor health.

The one weakness a buffalo has is a lack of resistance to stomach worms. Because they are now confined to a pasture, rather than roaming a wide prairie, they are exposed to these intestinal parasites. The farmer must medicate against this health problem a couple of times a year, or his animals will not survive. It is that important. Farms that attempt to meet organic standards with buffalo can face disaster from this source. Buffalo are normally raised as Natural rather than Organic for this reason.

Keeping buffalo safe is a matter of keeping them in their pasture. Fencing cannot be taken for granted with a herd of buffalo and gates must be kept closed at all times. An escaped buffalo is a danger to traffic and property. He is in danger from those who protect life and property of people. Having good fencing and working equipment is an expense required by farms choosing to raise buffalo. Keeping hunters and dogs out of pastures can prevent problems from occurring. A younger buffalo herd may run from intruders, while a mature herd might well run after them.

There are two sayings about buffalo that are very true: "You can chase a buffalo anywhere he wants to go." and "You can make a buffalo do anything he wants to do." The farmer must first decide what needs to be done, then figure out how to make the buffalo want to do it. Giving grain to a buffalo is like giving ice cream to a kid. They didn't evolve eating it, and too much of it is not good for them - but they sure do love it! By giving the buffalo treats of sweet grain or range cubes, the farmer teaches the buffalo to come to him when he wants them. This is a lot easier than going out to "round them up". With proper planing, managing buffalo can be fairly easy.

Most farms slaughter at least some animals for food each year. Some of these are being culled from the herd as inadequate mothers, but most are excess young bulls whose job it is to support the farm. This meat may be available to friends, neighbors, and family who buy a quarter or side of the animal. Word of mouth is usually how news of this meat is spread. The farmer may occasionally advertise meat if he has excess animals.

In order to sell meat in retail cuts at farmers markets, health food stores, grocery stores, and restaurants, the animal is slaughtered at a USDA inspected plant. This can be a very expensive process, and can add substantial costs to the price of the meat. It is frequently an all day trip to take the animals to that plant, and another trip two weeks later to pick up the meat.

Buffalo producers must pay for the USDA inspection, although this service is provided free by the government for beef, pork, and chicken. The transportation costs, time of travel, and cost of inspection can add well over a dollar a pound to the meat, even before considering the costs of the actual process of slaughter, hanging, and wrapping. This is considered the cost of keeping America's food supply safe, and is more important than ever in today's world.

While the outstanding health properties and taste qualities of the buffalo meat cannot be matched by any other meat, possibly the most precious contribution that buffalo brings to the consumer is the opportunity to know these wonderful American animals and the farmers who raise them. The relationship between farm and consumer has been lost in today's society. They are being brought together again by the American Buffalo.

A senior hiking club visited the herd

Back to farm visitors.... Sometimes the visitors come in groups, schools, clubs, you name it. One regular group is the Plein Air Painters of the Ozarks who come to paint outside twice are year, spring and fall. Another of the most regular groups was the Torch Christian Home School. They came six or seven years in a row and they were wonderful. Roughly 150 people came to the farm with that group which was split up in two days.

Most often there are family groups that come and these typically go out to the creep pen to call the herd up. But if there are only two or three folks and they are feeling adventurous, we take the ATV's out to visit the herd. We don't get too close to the herd, but often Tootsie will come up to visit with us and to sniff people's hand.

Chief Glenna Wallace of the Eastern Cherokee Nation visiting the herd

Early on, we often went into the field in the Trooper, but these days there is seldom a vehicle to go out in. That was like a safari, especially for the children sitting in the back. When buffalo stick their heads in the window for treats it is funny to watch people's reactions.

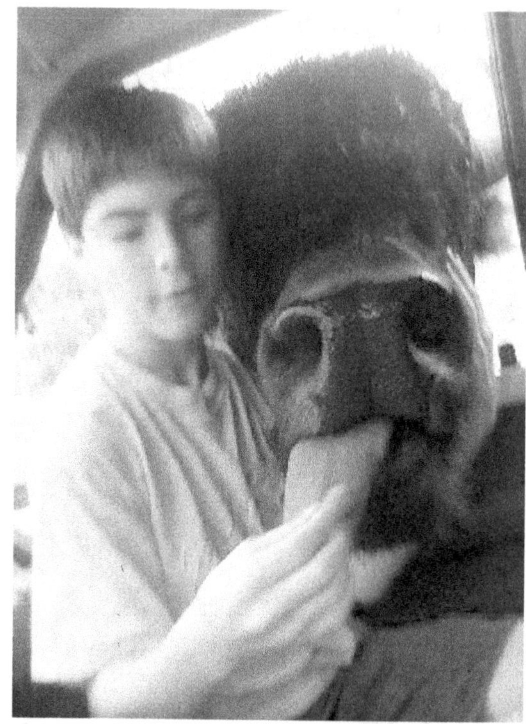

My nephews, Mike and Jamie, feeding buffalo range cubes from the Trooper

I remember one visit especially. A friend brought his son and two grandsons out to see the buffalo. One of the boys was afraid to go out in the Trooper so I asked him, 'did you see King Kong?' The boy nodded his head and his eyes got big. So I said 'George isn't that bad! Did you see Jaws?' again the nod, eyes bulging. 'Well George isn't that bad.' This went on until he was laughing and finally agreed to come along.

When we got into the field, George came up to the father's window in the front seat, took one look at his big beard and decided this was a bull he needed to take on. He hit the door with a mighty blow, then raked his horns up the side of the car. His horn caught the door handle and pulled the door open some. Then George lunged again which slammed the door shut. I drove away quickly so as not to give George another chance at the side of the car. The boys in the back seat were laughing because it happened to their father. Had George been at their window they probably would not have thought it was so funny.

Sometimes people are just passing through and want to see the buffalo. I encourage them not to use their GPS out in the boonies like this, or they are likely to be sent a VERY long way around. The farm is only a mile from the highway and with simple directions is easy to find.

One Native American couple visited from South Dakota. They saw buffalo every day –
but from a distance. When the buffalo were close enough to stick their head in the
window it was a new experience for them. It was beautiful that they burned an offering
of sweet grass smoke and sang a prayer chant for the buffalo. It was a very special
visit.

You are welcome to become a visitor to Oakcreek Buffalo Ranch. Just visit the website
at **www.ourbuffalofarm.com** for more information.

Chapter 20 People and Adventures

Bringing buffalo to our farm was a transforming event. Our whole life changed. We were outside so much more and bought the ATV's to get around the farm. The décor of the house changed from hand crafted items to bronzes, photos and pictures of buffalo. The lake house we had built to go to relax and get away from home was seldom visited, as we were having a more enjoyable time being outside at home with the herd. I still had to take long trips to do trade shows for the woodworking, but my heart was no longer in it.

I was more than willing to travel if there were bison to visit. There is a rapport between buffalo people because we are all interested in the same things and speak the same language – Buffalo. Besides having the herd, the people who have come into our lives are the most important change. We have been led to many wonderful and interesting places as well.

I have just returned from the International Bison Conference in Big Sky Montana. As I looked around the room at the six hundred people there, I only knew maybe fifty of them. But that left five hundred and fifty friends that I had not met yet. Over the course of the conference I was to meet many of those folks and hear the story of their farm and lives. From Australia to Canada and from all corner of the US they came, even a smattering of Europeans. I am so happy to have had that trip before finishing this book so that I could share the experience with you in the concluding chapters.

I headed to the Conference alone by truck, knowing I would be retracing steps I had traveled before. My first stop after a full day of traveling was at Custer, South Dakota in the Black Hills. I would visit Mount Rushmore at a time of year when the tourists were out in force. It was amazing how many people from around the world had congregated there at one time. What I really was there to see was Custer State Park.

Custer State Park is home to a very large and important bison herd numbering over two thousand. In an amazing feat, the herd there is 'rounded up' each fall. Cows over ten years old and many of the calves born that year will be auctioned off. It has been the source of breeding seed stock for many herds, including my friends Mike and Janie. They had submitted sealed bids back in 1994 for ten heifer calves. In March of 1995, Mike traveled out to Custer with a trailer to bring back those ten girls.

Leon and I were pretty excited to see the roundup that fall, and invited others to go with us. Janie had not seen the park before and was as excited about the trip as I was. Mike stayed home to look after their herd so their daughter Darla joined us. George and Lee Allen, friends from California joined the crew, as did my own mother from Florida. We were seven strong in the Chevy Van, but it held us all comfortably. We traveled the same route that I recently traveled to Big Sky. I am getting to know the way quite well, having been to the roundup three times now. I had called ahead for reservations at some cabins, but the owner said he did not know if he would still be there. If he was, he would make us a deal. We stayed there in three cabins for $20 each and enjoyed it immensely.

The round up exceeded our imagination. You would see a helicopters in the distance and knew it was keeping track of the herd. For weeks the herds were being hazed toward the south end of the park that housed the corrals. Horses and riders and trucks would be moving the herd toward the corral this morning. At last you saw the buffalo in the distance as they began streaming over the sides of the hills. They came closer and closer, then were running right by us. Later a fence was added to keep people back, but that first time we were there, there was nothing but grass between us and the buffalo.

As thrilling as this sight was for us, it was only the beginning of the show. For the next

three days, the herd would be worked through the squeeze chutes where they would be branded with the last number of the year they were born, wormed, vaccinated, and sorted. We could sit in bleachers or stand on a catwalk to look down on the action. A tractor with metal wings on front moved the animals forward from the pens a few at a time to enter the working area. It was more buffalo than I had ever seen in my life and I was enjoying every minute of it.

The cold wind that morning was bothering my mother's ears – so I bought her the only hat that was available at the concession stand. It had horns. She officially became our buffalo mascot. People stopped to take her picture and a local reporter interviewed her for the news. When she returned home, it became a favorite play game for her great grandchildren.

Once in September, I was coming home from a trade show in Reno and was making tracks for the roundup in the Black Hills. I spent the night on top of that hill where we watched the buffalo from, alone with the stars. It was spectacular! The back seat of the van made a queen sized bed for me and the static electricity every time I moved the sleeping bag looked like stars from the sky were exploding around me. That was a wonderful trip to and one of the other times I attended the roundup.

The National Bison Association has an Annual Conference and Gold Trophy Show and Sale in January each year. Then in the summer there is a meeting 'somewhere' across the country. Leon and I headed for Gillette, Wyoming one summer for the conference to be held there. The field day saw us loading into buses to visit a large ranch right out into the range with the buffalo.

This was new territory for me. That part of Wyoming was a vast plains where buffalo used to roam by the millions. That rancher explained to us that they practiced 'holistic management' with the herd and as a result could run a cow/calf pair on 35 acres. It used to take 50 acres for a cow calf pair. What??? This was a large herd and the ranch was huge.

I can run a cow/calf pair on a single acre in a good year, but we plan on two or three

acres for a cow/calf pair. We paid $1000 per acre for the new farm across the road, so it would cost us around $2500 to house a cow/calf pair. How much did land cost out in Wyoming? At $100 per acre, they would still be paying more than us. And with a ranch that large, how would they even FIND the herd. And just think how much fencing they would need to do..... I'm appreciating my own farm about then. And look at the picture. There is not a tree in sight. I love trees. Don't think I'll be moving out here anytime soon.

It was an education though to see the ranch and the sophisticated working facilities they used for the herd. The conference program was also educational for us and we enjoyed browsing through the trade show.

While we were visiting in Wyoming, it was just a short trip over to see Yellowstone for the first time. On the way, we stopped at the Little Big Horn battleground. What an awe inspiring place! It was just like it had been the day of the battle and white stones marked a place where a soldier's body was found. Custer was near the top of the hill

surrounded by some of his soldiers. It seemed like if you were quiet and listened, you would hear the sounds of the battle. You saw and heard it in your mind. The new monument to the Indians who fought there was inspirational as well when I recently visited.

We entered Yellowstone for the first time through the North entrance at Gardner. It was like entering a wonderland. Here we were at over 7000 feet altitude and there was a HUGE lake. It was hard to comprehend.

There were an amazing number of people visiting

in the park during the summer months. When an animal was spotted, cars would stop along the side of the road to look and take pictures. We saw lots of buffalo, one bear in the distance, a moose in the distance and plenty of elk. The scenery was breathtaking.

All of this was worth the trip to Yellowstone, but the most truly amazing thing of all was the geologic activity. Old Faithful gets lots of attention, but it was nothing compared to the geyser valley. Oh, my. Steaming water was spraying everywhere, weird colors in the water that was hot and bubbling. If you stepped off the walkways, you would quite possibly die from burns. Below the ground lurked molten rocks of a volcano. It was other worldly.

Years later on my way back from the trade show in Reno, I stopped at that geyser valley again in late September. I was on the walkway out in the middle of that spooky valley and there was not another living sole in sight. Big juicy flakes of snow began falling from the sky. What a difference from the crowds that had been here in summer. This world was suddenly all mine.

I asked a Japanese tourist to take my photo at the geyser valley.

One of the many rivers flowing from Yellowstone

On my 2017 trip to the International Bison Conference in Big Sky, I entered through the Eastern gate from Cody. I had stopped at the Buffalo Bill Museum there in Cody and could have spent days just browsing through that museum. If I head that way again in the future, I will have to leave myself more time in that town. Going into Yellowstone, I was really impressed with the rivers that were running out of that area in all directions, but the lake was so huge, it didn't make a dint in it. There must be an awful lot of snow falling in the winter here. I had only gone a mile or so when a buffalo bull crossed the road a few cars in front of me. Needless to say, traffic stopped for him. Then he just stood there like a Walmart greeter welcoming everyone to the park.

My last comment about the trip to Yellowstone is about the bison herds. They congregate in Hayden Valley for the rut in summer. Not only did the tourists stop, they went way out in the valley to take photos of the herd, even taking children with them. Apparently they were not aware of how fast a buffalo can charge and that the bulls are very protective of their cows they are trying to mate. Its no wonder that people get hurt by wildlife in the park.

Another year, the National Bison Association's summer conference went East to Kentucky. I was traveling alone to that event. We were given a list of bison farms that could be visited along the way and I was looking forward to that. You can always get ideas on visits to other farms and it is something I always recommend to other producers and those thinking of raising bison.

On one particular stop, I got really wonderful information about electric fencing, and since that was what we would soon be doing at home was the best thing I learned that summer. Where there are trees they are often used as fence posts. Between rocks and rugged terrain, we would be using lots of trees.

This farmer had cut treated 2x4s in half to make 2x2s. He cut these at five feet. This would provide for insulating three trees. In our air conditioned shop, we attached the insulators to the boards and pre-drilled them so they could be nailed to the tree. The shorter end pieces were used when the tree was not straight.

We did all our fencing this way and it saved countless hours of work in the field. All it took to attach these boards to the tree was three spikes nailed through pre-drilled holes, less than a minute for each tree. A visiting conservation officer said it was the best idea he had seen for electric fencing.

At another farm, we discovered that cities will give away used street sweeper brushes for free and they make excellent rubs for the bison. Simply put a post in the ground and slip the brush over the post using the tractor. When the animals rub on the brush, they leave wool behind to be easily collected. And the ladies really like grooming themselves on these brushes.

One trip that we seldom missed was to the auctions. It took us many years to get to be comfortable taking our own animals to auction after that disastrous auction where we brought our animals back home again. But that did not mean that we were not at the auctions ourselves. It was always exciting and fun to see friends. We didn't miss many.

One January, Leon and I went to the Gold Trophy Show and Sale in Denver. We watched the most beautiful buffalo in the world come into that ring. Bidding was wild and ended with that bull bringing a whopping $103,000. Wow! But he was worth every penny of it. I can't imagine any buffalo ever being finer than he was. If the buyer bred him to twenty cows with a premium added of $5000 each for calves being sired by him, they would get their money back in only a year or two. But things happen..... He was so gorgeous that he attracted lightening. At ten years of age, he was struck by lightening and killed. So sad!

I was elected president of the Missouri Bison Assertions two years in a row and felt it was my obligation to support the auctions rather than selling from the farm those two years. To my surprise, auction prices were skyrocketing and the calves brought more at the auction than I would have charged at home.

In 2017, six 350 pound bull calves that I brought to the auction brought $2000 each. The one heifer calf brought $1500. It will be hard for the buyers to make much money selling meat when paying those prices and still needing to feed them for nearly two more years before they are big enough to process. But it will guarantee supply in the future and it is getting harder and harder to find animals to fill the demand. For the heifer, she is worth the price to the meat suppliers unfortunately. For someone wanting quality breeding stock, they will need to up their price to get ahead of the meat market.

International Bison Conferences are being held every five years, sometimes in the States and other times in Canada. 2017 was the first one I had attended but it is not likely to be the last. It was WONDERFUL! The Big Sky Resort was bursting at the

seams with six hundred adults and seventy five children registered for the conference.

The conference kicked off on the 4th of July when we headed by bus to the nearby 320 Ranch. There we had a drone demo, our first speakers and good food and wonderful concert by Michael Martin Murphy. I also experienced my first virtual reality glasses and I was hooked. I ordered a pair on Amazon as soon as I got home and can't wait to give them a try. I had lunch with a couple from Australia. It was really interesting to hear about animals and agriculture in that country. They were to receive their first bison in two weeks and were excited. Other Australians stopped by the table as well. Even though these were to be the first bison in Australia, they had already formed a Bison Association. The buses returned us to Big Sky in time for the firework display.

We heard presentations on Bison in a Changing Climate, herd health issues, marketing, holistic management, and food preparation and so on. We ate well to say the least. Western Bison Company's bison hot dogs deserved special mention though, they were the best I had ever eaten. And I really enjoyed the Wylie And the Wild West Concert.

Also deserving my special mention was a presentation by Jessie Price, editor of EatingWell Magazine, along with Adam Danforth, a James Beard Award Winning Author/Butcher, and Kyle Mendenhall, Chef from Arcana Restaurant in Bolder. Jessie brought us up to date on America's eating trends and moderated the interaction between butcher and chef. Adam cut meats before us, then Kyle prepared those meats. The resort chefs cooked the meats over Big Green Egg barbecues and passed samples around for everyone to taste. It was one of the best presentations ever, even if we were under a tent with rain coming down outside.

The conference kicked off a special plan for the future of the buffalo when they announced a long term push to more than double the number of bison in the world to more than one million in ten years, by 2027.

This week, the National Bison Association announced a new campaign called "Bison 1 Million" at the International Bison Conference in Big Sky, Montana. The group—with the support of its Canadian counterpart, the Intertribal Buffalo Council, and the Wildlife Conservation Society—hopes to introduce and improve upon practices to bring the bison back at scale.

That is a plan that I can get behind whole-heartedly. It is ambitious to be sure, as it means that we need more people to raise buffalo and more people to eat it. Eating bison is the only way to ensure its economic importance and enable farmers and ranchers to afford to raise more buffalo. A Campaign was kicked of to make every Wednesday not just 'hump day', but 'Bison Hump Day', encouraging folks to eat bison.

*Day 3 of the IBC - the MoBA contingency! Spending time with these
wonderful folks enjoying an amazing experience!
I was delighted to see that nearly half our folks from Missouri were under 35*

The best part of the conference for me was the visit by bus to Ted Turner's beautiful
ranch. Over seven thousand buffalo roamed the ranch. The sight filled my heart.
Someone later asked me if I thought that is what the country used to look like. I
thought it over and replied, 'No, its what we hope the future looks like.'

As you can tell, I am enthusiastic about the future of bison, more so than I have ever
been. I'll be doing my part to help make One Million Bison a reality in my lifetime.

Chapter 21 Joining the Herd

Buffalo are wonderfully independent and head strong. You can't make them do anything they don't want to do. Well, folks who raise buffalo are a lot like that too. And like the buffalo, we have learned that there are real advantages in being with a herd.

When Leon and I got our first buffalo girls, there was no Missouri Bison Association. We went to the sales in Kansas and Oklahoma as well as the National Bison Association in Denver. We relied on the NBA for information as well as the people we met along the way. The NBA has a Bison Breeders Handbook and a Bison World magazine that was quite valuable as well. I was hungry for anything I could learn about bison.

A year or two later, the Missouri Bison Association was formed and Leon and I quickly became involved. We hosted one of the early meetings at our farm which allowed us to get to know our fellow producers better. I guess the association was really eager too, because instead of hosting just one auction in the Fall of the year, we added one in the Spring as well.

The auctions are a lot of work for the board members, but they bring out many people to the event who are members or become members while there. MoBA always hosts a complimentary meal the evening before and a meeting to keep everyone up to date on the industry. The sales also provide most of the revenue needed to keep the organization going and to keep membership costs low at $35 per year. The NBA dues can be cost prohibitive for some folks, so we are proud to keep our dues low.

A newsletter was started called The Quarterly Grunt. After a few years, I became the editor of that newsletter. The name of Quarterly was removed at that point as I was producing an eight page newsletter six or seven times a year and enjoying the process. I refused an elected office as I felt that I had enough influence on the organization as editor.

My friend Janie and I had attended lots of NBA conferences and we felt that we were ready to try our wings at organizing one here for our membership. We started with a one day event the day before the fall sale and included a lunch as well as dinner. There was no cost, the organization would pay for it. But we do have a 'fun auction' after each dinner, where folks donate items to be auctioned off. If almost always paid for the dinners.

Janie and I also enjoyed preparing an outstanding meal before one of the auctions. I cooked the bison lasagna for over sixty folks that day. We made a great team and were ready to go bigger with the conference idea. We planned the next conference to be in Joplin at the Holiday Inn, organized speakers for the event, planned meals and a field day to be held at Oakcreek Buffalo Ranch the following day. Over sixty people were registered for the event and it was a great success.

Its funny to look back and see how quickly Janie and I became the 'experts' in raising bison to new folks getting in the bison business. We both gave presentations at that conference. Janie's presentation was on agri-tourism and mine was Bison Behavior and Management and I have included it below.

Bison Behavior and Management

Understanding Bison Behavior and Characteristics for Effective Herd Management

Raising Buffalo is 90% planning and 10% work. That's not to say that there is not work involved, but compared to the management of other animals, it is minimal. In order to plan effectively, you must know your animals and the current status of the herd.

Buffalo watching is not a spectator sport-- it's your job. Learn to observe: study the herd, the condition of individual animals, effect of the seasons, the pasture and fence. Use your eyes and your mind to know every detail of your animals and their environment. Assess any improvements or changes that need to be made. Plan ahead for the coming seasons. Your goal should be to avoid problems rather than fix them. These skills will add to your effectiveness as a farmer, and add to your interest and satisfaction with the job.

Understanding the Nature of Buffalo*: Buffalo are wild animals. There is not a tame or domesticated hair on their head. You can gain their trust and friendship, but you have not really changed their basic nature----they will always be wild. This free and independent nature is a strong part of the appeal buffalo have to us. There is only one way to make a buffalo do anything, and that is to make him want to do it. Forget everything you know about cattle. These animals have a nature all their own, and that is what you will try to come to know and understand. It is that independent nature that will affect the ways which you manage your herd.*

Everything in life is a trade-off. As you come to win the acceptance of your animals, they will lose their fear of you. That will eliminate many problems of control, but will create other problems in their place. Their new proximity to you will create new dangers as well. Always stay safe. Farming is a dangerous occupation at best, especially with equipment and animals. If you are hurt by your buffalo, the animal will get the blame for your mistake, and you will be labeled a fool for having them on your farm in the first place.

Being in the middle of a buffalo herd is no place for a person. You may think they like and accept you. Look close at how they interact with each other. They like each other, but they still act very violently with their buddies. They butt and gouge at each other, and you will notice that the receiver of that action takes the threat/danger very seriously. They avoid being trapped by any animal more dominant than they, and stay our of their space. If they make a mistake, they are promptly and harshly reminded of their place.

If you want to be a part of the herd, you will also be in their pecking order---and they will find out that you should be on the bottom rung. The bull will test you first, and there may not be enough left for any of the others to play with. Sp if you don't want an affectionate buffalo jumping on your butt, then stay on the other side of the fence. Otherwise, you will learn all about tough love. Your reaction times are not good enough to avoid the actions of a buffalo.

Buffalo are athletic animals:
 Fast---they have incredible reaction times and outrun horses
 Turn on a dime---very dexterous
 Good jumpers---and good kickers (need I say more?)
 Good swimmers
 Strong---about four times stronger than cows
 Wild---they use their athletic abilities and stay in condition

Buffalo are perfectly adapted to their environment:

1) HAIR They have 8 times as many hair follicles than cattle. This gives them an exceptional advantage over cattle in extreme cold environments of Northern latitudes. Yet they have the amazing ability to shed those hairs in the summer to adapt to heat. There are commercial uses for that hair which have the potential for expanded producer profits.

2) METABOLISM In order to adapt to the change of seasons, the metabolism of bison slows in winter. This decreases their feed intake at a time when grass is unavailable and supplements expensive. This represents a benefit to the producer, unless he happens to be feeding bulls for slaughter. That producer will be frustrated by the lack of growth of his animals in winter. Relax. Nature says this is the best *adaptation. Accept and enjoy it.*

3) LONG LIFE SPAN *Bison grow slowly. They are small when born, usually 35 to 50 lbs. This helps prevent calving problems. They mature slowly, usually calving for the first time at three years of age. This means extra time and expense when starting a herd. But they live and reproduce for 20 to 30 years. This long breeding life means fewer replacement heifers, and overall, a productive and economical animal to raise.*

4) RUTTING SEASON *Like deer, bison have a rutting season, only in late summer rather than fall. The gestation period is nine months, so babes are born in April through June when grass in at its optimum growth and nutrition for the nursing mothers and the*
 calves who are learning to graze.

5) GRAZING ANIMALS *Bison evolved on GRASS not GRAIN. As a result, they have a more efficient digestive system than cattle on forage. When fed a higher quality diet, cows do as well as bison. But on marginal forage, bison convert protein better. Because of their higher economic value, producers tend to not take advantage of this quality, and give them the best feed possible. As prices for bison fall, many producers may come to have a greater appreciation of the digestive system of bison.*

BISON BEHAVIOR
Buffalo have an extremely strong herd instinct.
Buffalo have strong sense of personal self and self preservation
Bison relate to each other through a strict pecking order. Any discussion of behavior is colored by the perceptions of the observer. It not as "cut and dried" a science as physical characteristics. So as I present this part of the session, please understand that this is my own observations, and that other people may not agree with all of my assertions.

HERD INSTINCTS: *Buffalo tend to stay very close together, whether for protection or for social contact. They react to danger as a group, first to flee and then to return out of curiosity to see what "spooked" them. They react first, then ask questions later. They come to the aid of any member of the herd that is in distress. Yet, ironically, they will attack an injured member of the herd and can cause serious damage or even death to that animal. They have close "family" ties with other herd members, but will not hesitate to inflict punishment on those who violate their "space".*

SELF PRESERVATION: *Bison will protect themselves first, whether by fleeing or fighting. Defending other herd members seems to be an extended sense of self preservation. If grain or range cubes is presented, the animals will compete for as* *much as they can possibly get for themselves. They will push aside any animal less dominant than themselves with no attempt to share with other members of the herd. The weaker members of the herd will not fight the stronger ones to get food, even though they want the grain just as strongly as the others. Middle animals will eat as fast as they can, to get as much as they can, before the stronger ones push them away. They then run to another space where they see someone less dominant than themselves to push away. Calves enjoy the same position in the herd as their mother, as she will defend their rights.*

PECKING ORDER: *Social order within the herd is very strict. It is their way of balancing the good of the herd with the will of the individual. It is a definite hierarchy, with the strongest animals at the top, and the weakest at the bottom. Although the strong will defend the weak, the strong also get the best of everything available. It definitely is not share and share alike. This insures that the strongest will not only survive, but will be in the best condition to breed. When determining the value of any animal within the herd, I let the animals themselves tell me who is the superior animal.*

The strongest bull will be the most dominant animal in the herd. But the dominant cow will be the leader of the herd. The bull's job is protection and breeding. He is too busy doing those things to be bothered with the everyday decisions of the herd. So the female takes over to have the most influence on the activities of the herd. The most dominant, however, is not always the natural leader in all instances. The herd will follow specific individuals whose judgment they like, rather than always following the strongest female. Likewise, the cows will choose the bull with whom they will breed. If she does not like to dominant bull, she will not permit him to breed her.

It is necessary for the bull to seriously court every female he wishes to breed, every time he wished to breed her. Often the bull is busy courting a cow, and another cow will come into season. A younger bull will do the courting of the new cow while the big guy is busy. But after the dominant bull has taken the original cow, he will come courting the now ripe female and soon take her affections from the young bull. Frequent conflicts will occur within the herd as members attempt to move up their position in the hierarchy of the herd. They know the value of every step up that they can accomplish.

PERSONALITY: *Each animal has its own personality. Much of this is inherited from its parents, much is learned from its mother and other members of the herd, and its own experiences color its behavior. They also have "good days" and "bad days" just like you and I. The personality of individuals in turn make up the "herd personalities". Any maladjusted animals should be culled from the herd or they will in turn affect well being of the rest of the animals, and could be a danger to the producer and the public.*

Because of my close relationship to my herd, I tend to become attached to those with the most pleasant behavior and keep their offspring. But if you are weaning the babe of your "best friend cow", she is not going to be your buddy and behave as she normally would. Remember, always be careful!

PERSONALITY CHARACTERISTICS OF BISON: *The nature of bison is that they are friendly and curious. They have little to fear from the world, and are defensive of their territory from natural predators. Their self assurance increases with age and their position with in the herd. Their extremely quick reaction times compensate for the generally placid nature of the animals.*

They are playful, and at times even seem to have a sense of humor. Trust is not easily given, and you will have to earn their friendship. They do not hold grudges, and will soon forgive you for the insult you do when working them. Whether it is from an innate sense of stubbornness or independence, buffalo will only do what they want to do, and cannot be "made" to do things. Save your self frustration and grief, and try to figure out how to make the animals "want" to do what you want them to. (a hint is that this is easiest accomplished using food.)

MANAGEMENT DECISIONS *There are management decisions in raising bison which will have to be made by each producer. Management philosophies and practices differ widely within the industry. Time may not be adequate for presentations of these important factors. They will be touched on here for reference. Management practices range across a broad field: One producer may dehorn all his buffalo, feed grain, wean babes, rotational graze, use only young bulls, and remove bulls from the herd in the fall. Another producer may run his herd in family groups using older bulls which are always with the herd, naturally wean babes, not dehorn, and grass feed only. Each producer should look at these management practices and decide for himself which works for his own farm and philosophy.*

TO DEHORN OR NOT TO DEHORN: *Producers who de-horn their animals tell me that it is the best decision they could have made. I have yet to talk to one who has told me that he regrets de-horning his herd. Among the reasons for dehorning is safety for the animal and the handler. Another is for preventing damage to hides as the buffalo fight flies.*

Producers who do not dehorn wish to preserve the animal in its natural state. They are willing to take the risk of injury to self and animal to "let buffalo be buffaloes". Those who do dehorn will usually not dehorn animals that they plan to sell. It reduces the number of potential buyers for that animal, and they do not show as well at auctions resulting in lower prices. The number of producers who do not dehorn are in the majority, but a lot of that may be due to lack of any decision. My head may tell me to dehorn, but at this point, my heart would not let me.

WEANING: *Do you take the babes away from their mothers, or wait for the mother to accomplish that job herself? There is little doubt that the buffalo mom could do a perfectly fine job without any help from us. Will it help her to breed back if you remove the calf? No, she breeds back in roughly three months, long before anyone would wean the calf. But the producer must make economic decisions---does he need to sell those babes at a fall or early spring auction? Does he have room for additional animals in his pastures? A long range plan for the offspring needs to be developed (and be flexible as conditions change).*

CREEP FEEDING *Supplementing grain in creep feeders for calves is an important consideration. Is it a necessity? NO. Is it a good practice? Maybe. So, yes or no? I have decided "yes, in moderation". Too much is a waste of money, and could be detrimental to the health of the babes. A little could help the babes reach their genetic potential, and do so at a faster pace than otherwise possible. It could take some of the pressure off the mothers as they go into the breeding season, helping them to be in peak condition. At our farm, the creep pen is a valuable tool for weaning the babes. In our industry, a lot of emphasis is put on having large calves at weaning and at the fall auctions. This can only be accomplished by three things: a) early calving b) genetics and c) creep feeding. The only way you can truly attribute large size to genetics is to visit the herd that the calves came from. Creep feeding can be a mask for quality. The feeding can be beneficial when the babes are stressed by weaning, helping to keep them healthy and happy. It is a valuable tool. How you chose to use it is up to you.*

ROTATIONAL GRAZING: *To use the land available to its fullest potential will without doubt require a plan of rotational grazing. It will provide an estimated 40% increase in the amount of grass available. But what will be buffalo think of all that control? After all they are independent, and roam throughout their territory at will. Trust me, if they object too strongly, they will let you know by rearranging the fences. The field they are being moved to should be better than the one they are leaving, and they will be eager for the new territory. So they will move readily when needed, and stay where they are put as long as the grazing is good.*

More management and fencing are needed on the part of the producer, and the labor must be available when needed. What sold me on the "idea" of rotational grazing was the better quality and quantity of grass available for the animals. If they could vote, they would probably vote to rotate. It could also provide a stockpile of grass well into the winter for better economics and nutrition. And Animals may be allowed to have full run of the pastures as the winter progresses. It is definitely a plan worth considering for both better economics of the farm and for the well being of the animals.

GRAIN FEEDING*: Probably the most controversial management practice in the bison industry today is whether or not to feed grain to bison. Following World War 2, cattle producers began feeding excess grain to beef herds. As ranchers began raising bison, many of them followed the same practices being used to raise beef. But the animals are totally different. And even beef did not evolve eating grain---they are grazing animals.*

Now, producers have to decide for themselves whether or not it makes good sense for them to grain feed their own animals. Our cow herd has not received any grain supplements for three years. They graze on a grass and clover (and weeds!) pasture, and their condition is so good that they simply do not need any supplemental feeds, only mineral and hay as required.

To feed them grain would be the same as over watering a houseplant: it would detrimental to their well-being and to our pocketbook. Feeding bulls before slaughter will speed the process of growing to slaughter size. This will be offset by the additional cost of the grain. It will affect the fat deposits in the animal, both in the amount and type of fat. Even with grain feeding, bison will have a more healthy, nutritious meat that is lower in fat.

The nutrition of a grass fed animal is definitely superior. Is the tenderness or taste better in grain fed animals? Everyone has their own opinion on the subject. Unfortunately, it is one of the things we will have to decide for ourselves. Grain feeding is closely associated with feed lots, and therefore with antibiotics and growth hormones - and with quality of life issues for the animals. At all costs, my opinion is that feedlot situations are best avoided. But I refuse to tell others how to run their farms, in hopes that they will let me operate mine as I see best. We can best influence other producers with our example and success, and keep conflicts from injuring our industry.

Those attending the conference provided their own transportation to the farm the following day. Leon and I both enjoyed showing the working equipment and animals that day and there were many questions. I served my Lasagna A LA Harold that day to a very appreciative bunch of people. Karen Conley from the North American Bison Journal was present at the conference and wrote a four page article about the event. An interview with me was the centerfold. I was impressed!

Also present at the conference and field day was Lance Gegner of ATTRA.

Lance subsequently published a Bison Production Guide for that organization in which my presentation was quoted often. That publication is still available online at https://attra.ncat.org/attra-pub/viewhtml.php?id=252

Leon and I were married for 43 years. Because he was twenty years older then me, I always assumed that some day I would be without him. But when he passed away in 2010, it was harder on me than I had expected. I withdrew from involvement in many activities, including the bison association and passed the newsletter on to someone else.

The bison seemed to be aware that something was wrong. A few nights after Leon had passed away, a car pulled into the driveway at two a.m. I was not asleep and saw the lights. A man at the door asked "is this the buffalo farm? There is a buffalo down on the creek. Are you alone? We'll help you. We'll try to haze him back in this direction."

I quickly dressed and jumped on the four wheeler. As I headed down the road, I saw the lights of his truck coming toward me, but they turned on to a side road. I went to the intersection and waited. About ten minutes later the truck returned and said the bull was in the old chicken house by the neighbor's house where the yard light was. I went there and saw him running around by all the equipment that was stored inside. There was no front to the building and I could not lock him.

I decided to try to lead him home although I had no food for him with me. I called him and motioned for him to come – and he did! I led him back to the gravel road, but he turned in the wrong direction.... Now I was racing him at full speed to try to turn him back but could not get ahead of him. The road dead ended and I stopped. He went around the barrier and stopped to, waiting for me to come with him. No, I told him, I'll see you in the morning.

John, my tenant in the hundred year old farmhouse, and I hunted for him the next morning with no luck. We found where the fence was down for him to get out and made the repairs. The herd was in the woods and it was impossible for me to see how many were there or missing. Later that day when I went out to check, the bull was laying in the middle of the herd, acting quite innocent. Apparently he had gone back in the say way he had come out.

Two days later, John called and said there was a bull laying OUTSIDE the gate to the pasture. I went to check and it was the second biggest bull. The herd was right inside the gate. I opened the gate and he got up and walked back in. He had been out all that time as well.

Four years later, I was attending the Spring auction and sat in on a board meeting of MoBA. The officers would be unable to serve the coming year and they had no one to replace them. In order to keep the association going, I had no choice but to accept the position of President and try to recruit new members to serve as officers and board members that evening. New people accepted the call. I had the best people with me that I possibly could have found! I also became the newsletter editor once more.

We accepted the request to have another conference. It had been ten years since MoBA had had a conference. We were ambitious in our planning, with a three day conference at the beautiful Downstream Casino west of Joplin. We had speakers the first day and then spent the following two days taking buses to visit farms and a processing plant. People were there from as far away as Canada and Georgia.

We hosted a booth at Farmfest in Springfield each year in the cattle barn. People would be looking at cattle and come around the corner face to face with a HUGE bison

shoulder mount. It looked like he was alive. He was definitely a show stopper. Keith Ashton and I manned the booth all three days and had a blast. Others worked with us when they could get there. It kept bison in the mind of potential bison producers and helped get farmers to consider adding bison to their operations. At the same time we encouraged consumers to try bison meat and told about the health benefits.

When my two year term as president of MoBA expired, I left the organization in fine, very capable hands. Even the newsletter was passed to a new editor. I still write articles for that paper but leave the editing, printing and mailing to other folks. The association website at www.mobisonassoc.org was also left in more capable hands than mine.

If any reader is interested in raising bison, my best advice would be to look for your state's bison association. If you don't find one, look to a neighboring state. You can find the National Bison Association at www.bisoncentral.com. Look for buffalo farms near you and give them a call. I am sure you will be pleasantly surprised by your friendly reception.

Chapter 22   Lessons Learned

Twenty two years have passed since that Friday the 13th back in 1995 when the first fifteen buffalo babes arrived. There have been many learning experiences along the way. None have been disastrous, thank goodness, but some certainly could have been. I count myself blessed to be able to say this now.

Probably the most important lesson learned was that it is easier to prevent problems than to fix them after they have occurred. An example that comes to mind right away is having the veterinarian out to work calves. The babes got wound up and hit a gate. I was dismayed to witness the gate spring open and half a dozen babes escape into the pasture. Had I taken the time to simply loop a chain around that gate before starting to work the animals, it is doubtful that they would have gotten away.

As it was, we worked the remaining babes and had the veterinarian come back a few days later to work the escapees. We were tagging their ears, injecting wormer and vaccinations. By locking the worked babes in one pen with food, and opening the gate to the pasture, the escapees came back into the pen to get their share of the food. It was easy to lock them in again.

The second lesson learned is that if you goof in your planning, the buffalo will know – and they will soon show you where the problem was. And lastly, when you plan, make sure that there are safeguards in place so that if something does go wrong, both you and the buffalo will still be safe and secure. In the example above, there were no other buffalo in the pasture where the babes escaped into and all gates to that pasture were closed. That made it safer for us when we were working the babes, and easier to retrieve the escapees. Had those gates been open, the escapees might well have joined the herd again, with no way to get them back without sorting the whole herd.

My buffalo are used to me and we get along really well – until I try to make them do something they don't want to do. That is when their wild nature comes out. The old saying holds true even with a herd that is used to people: You can make a buffalo do anything he wants to do. So the trick is to always try to figure out how to make the buffalo want to do what you want them to do. Hint, using food works best. Sometimes the buffalo win.... That makes it challenging and interesting. They really are smart.

A friend was visiting one day along with her son who was home from Desert Storm where he worked on Apache helicopters. He commented on the baby buffalo out in the far side of the pasture from the house. I told him there were no babes yet this year, but he insisted that he saw one. We jumped on the bikes to check it out and sure enough here was the first new babe of the year, a little bull that we christened Apache.

Many months later, we were moving calves across the road to the corral and had

Apache in the creep pen to move. That night I woke to the dogs raising a ruckus in the yard. I looked out the window and saw a buffalo chasing the dogs around the front yard. Apache has escaped the pen next to where the trailer was backed up and he was not happy.

I went rushing down the stairs and out into the yard to open the nearest gate. When Apache saw me, he came charging at me. In the dark of night, he looked huge and ferocious and I had no place to hide. As he charged toward me, I threw up my hand and shouted NO! To my surprise, he stopped. I lost a shoe in my rush, but I motioned for him to follow me as I headed to the gate. He watched and when the gate was open, in he went.

The next day, Apache came into the creep pen again and was once more caught. He was moved across the road in the trailer with no further incidents. What really surprised me was that he had now become my buddy, eating out of my hand and coming to me when ever I visited the babes. Seems that by letting him back into the pasture, he had come to trust me. For me, it was one of the first times I ever had to try to 'buffalo' a buffalo – kind of like calling their bluff. He could have destroyed me, and I had no option but to stand up to him. That seemed to win his respect. My but he was a fine buffalo bull!

I an reqired to work more with the babes than with the rest of the herd and had some interesting experiences. Once when loading a heifer calf into the trailer to move her across the road, I pulled the trailer gate closed so hard that it got stuck without being able to lock it. In frustration, I decided that if I could not open it, I might as well take her to the corral before trying to pry it open. When I got to the corral, I found that the gate to the trailer was open and no babe inside. Oh, dear, it had jarred lose and the babe was gone. I looked back the way I had come and was surprised to see her running toward me. She was trying to keep up with the trailer.... I simply opened the gate into the corral and in she ran. It was like a miracle. She had gone right where I needed her to be. Bet that would not happen again in a million years.

Another time I had moved a bull and a heifer across the road to the corral pen and come back to the house to catch more babes. So the next day I went over to check on these two before moving more into the pen. But there was only ONE babe in the pen. The little girl was missing. How could she get out and the bull not? The herd was surrounding the pen, and I could see that whole pasture. She was not there. The only possible answer was that he had eaten her. Well, of course that had not happened, but where could she be? There had been ten babes in that pen for two weeks earlier and none had escaped back to their herd.

I locked the gate to keep the herd in the pasture where the corral was and went in search of the babe. I spotted her as far away as she could get from the corral. I opened the entry gate to the road and went to herd her toward it by tacking back and forth behind her on the bike. When she got to the open gate, she ran across the road, up the driveway and back around to the creep pen. I let her in the pen with the other babes and went back across the road to let the herd out of the corral pasture. BUT now the little bull was missing! Oh, there he was with the herd. Now how did he get out?

I was going to have to ponder on what to do next and was returning to the house. I looked behind me and he was following me. I led him back to the creep pen where his sister was and locked him in. When I went back to the corral pen, I discovered that the water course had a post that had been loosened and they had both pushed under it. I secured that area with more posts and was able to move the babes where they needed to be. It seemed like these babes were trying to co-operate with me given the chance. Sometimes its hard to figure out just what they are thinking, but I like that they respond to my behavior. Maybe they think of me as their surrogate mother.

Fortunately, buffalo prefer to take care of themselves rather than have me take care of them. I can work with that.... I wish the pasture could do the same thing. Its the pasture and fences that require taking care of. I've learned a LOT of lessons about land as well.

The view from the windows of our house are breathtaking. I would gaze over the tree covered hills and want to make it ALL MINE. Bur you know what they say, be careful what you wish for. Harold sold us the 117 acres across the road and we eagerly started fencing off the pastures. We fenced and we fenced. Then I broke my arm – at a buffalo auction no less. Fencing stopped at that point and somehow never started up again. Much of the perimeter fence was barb wire that only came up to my waist. It was years before that became a problem, but of course it was inevitable.

But fencing was just the start of the work on the new property. It had to be mowed regularly or it would grow up into woods again quickly. The hills were really steep in places and it was dangerous work. When the tractor slipped out of gear on one such slope, Leon had an exciting ride to the bottom. And he tried to turn the tractor to avoid going through a fence. That is how you can get a tractor to turn over on you. One neighbor had died that way before we moved here. I put my foot down. The slopes are welcome to grow back into woods again. They were no longer going to be mowed. Now that I realized how much work would be involved on owning larger parcels of land, I no longer wanted to own more. I would be content just to enjoy the view.

We attended grazing schools and learned about rotational grazing. If you stock the herd in small pastures, it allows the other pastures to rest and grow. This method of grazing can actually allow for maybe 40% more animals to be pastured on the land and still have better forage for the herd to eat.

With this in mind, we divided the new property into seven different pastures, each with access to water. Someone asked me 'How do you move the buffalo?' I wish every job was so easy, you simply open a gate. There is nothing a buffalo loves better than an open gate, its even better than food. Maybe that is because they will be looking for more food through the open gate.

All went well in the beginning, but as the herd grew and weather events happened, we were always having to repair the fence. If a wire touches the ground, it shorts out the whole fence. There were many places where the stream went under the fence and when the water got high, there went the fence again. If a tree fell – and there are lots of trees – there goes the fence again. I could tell when the fence was no longer hot. Members of the herd, often babes, would graze the tall grass under the fence. Their heads would brush against the fence and it would start swaying. Had it been hot, they would not have touched it. That was my warning unless I had a tester with me each time I checked on the herd.

Lightening strikes often killed the fence charger, and I had an $800 one. I had to finally give up on paying that kind of money for a charger that the lightening was going to get anyway. At one point, I even stopped replacing the charger and the fence was not hot for nearly two years. But then animals started going through it and the vacation was over. A new charger was a must and the fence had to be maintained.

In the winter, we opened the gates to all the pastures and let the herd graze where ever they wanted. What we found was that the herd went EVERYWHERE. There were no areas that were under grazed the way that cattle would do. And if we took out some of the cross fences, it would be easier for us to maintain. It was much harder to take out the fence than it had been to put in, but at least was not expensive. I did hire some college students to do that job for me.

Now there were only four pastures instead of seven. And the herd was permanently fenced out of one. There was not enough grazing in those woods to finish running the electric in that area or to maintain it. It made excellent hunting property, and many friends enjoyed that privilege, although Leon and I did not hunt.

Another lesson learned was that it was better to buy hay than to cut it from our own property. Those big round bales are very reasonably priced. In fact I'm paying about the same now as we did twenty years ago, roughly $30 per bale. And surprise, there is about $10 worth of fertilizer in each bale plus lots of organic matter. The buffalo eat the bales and scatter the fertilizer and organic matter all over the pastures as they graze, improving the soil. No expensive machinery required or labor to run it. The tractor only gets used to put the bales out in the winter.

When we mow the fields to remove weeds and seed heads, we leave the clippings right where they land, adding organic matter to be incorporated into the soil. I learned that when grazing animals take a bite of grass, the roots of that plant dies in the soil to the height of the remaining grass. As that grass grows taller again, new root growth keeps pace with the above ground growth. The root that died becomes organic matter for the microbes and earthworms to feast on and the soil is improved. This process also sequesters carbon in the soil, taken from the CO2 in the air, helping to control green house gases.

If the pasture is not mowed or grazed, the plants go to seed and then go dormant. If the vegetation is cut back and not allowed to go to seed, it stays in a vegetative state and provides more food of excellent quality for the animals.

There is a lot of lack of knowledge by the public and many folks believe that cattle produce methane during digestion and contribute to greenhouse gases. While this may be especially true in a feedlot environment, when the animals are grazing on pasture, they are enhancing the environment rather than damaging it. Think of the millions of bison that roamed America before they were nearly wiped out. They helped make the prairies as we found them.

Contrast grazing animals with farming grains and vegetables. The soils have become depleted of nutrients by continually being mined to grow plants. Soils are often tilled which in turns damages soil microbes and worms. Add chemical weed killers and pesticides used, and the soil becomes dead. It also washes away down the rivers to create a 'dead' area in the Gulf of Mexico. I personally think that meat production is on the whole much more environmentally friendly than much of agriculture.

Another lesson that I have learned over the years is that the Conservation Department is much more interested in the survival of wildlife than it is the financial success of the farm. There are many cost share programs for the farmer from this source. They will help you put in wells to keep animals out of waterways and ponds. And they are good at cost sharing fences to keep livestock out of the woods. They even help harvest trees from the woods which is an economic boon for the farmer.

Much emphasis is put on pasture grasses by the Conservation Department, and much work and cost goes into eradicating fescue grasses in favor of warm season grasses. This is primarily to provide nesting areas for birds and small animals rather than to improve grazing for ruminant animals like buffalo. There are many warm season grasses naturally in the field such as foxtail, bermuda, and crab grass. When the cool season grasses go dormant in the heat of summer, the warm season grasses happily step in to provide plenty of summer grazing. Killing off the fescue and orchard grasses also kills off the clovers and so forth. The result is less grazing available in Spring and Fall. I don't feel that the average beginning farmer who turns to conservation for help establishing pastures is getting the best assistance when it comes to pasture establishment. That is my personal opinion.....

Maybe the most important lesson for me is that I'm not getting any younger. When I reached 70, it was time to wonder how long I can keep raising buffalo? I knew what I wanted the answer to be – as long as I live. Leon was 70 when we got those first girls. The true answer was as long as I was able to. So I determined to make sure I stayed healthy and fit. That involved starting by losing 50 pounds. As I neared that goal, I realized that more was involved than just being thinner, I needed exercise to become fit. The results has been amazing as I feel better than I can even remember. Its wonderful! I should give credit here for a book that both educated me but also was motivating: Younger Next Year by Henry Lodge, MD and Chris Crowley. If you are looking for motivation to get in better shape, that is a fine place to turn.

Raising buffalo for twenty two years has been a good start. Now I'm ready for the next twenty two years.

Chapter 23   Into the Future

Small farms are becoming rare in this country. A Century ago, seventy percent of Americans lived on a farm. Today that has shrunk to a mere two percent. And on those remaining farms there are more of the farmers are over seventy than under thirty five. Family farms are at serious risk. Older farmers typically have no formal plan to transfer succession of ownership. Their lives are invested in their farm and they hang on to the management/ownership until health no longer allows.

Farmers have often used their farms as collateral and the land is heavily leveraged. In order to retire should they have the desire to do so, they need to ask full market price for the farm. This is out of reach for younger family members, so the land is swallowed up by large agricultural operations consolidating farmland in rural areas or, if the farm is in the shadow of a city, property developers. Another family farm bites the dust.

When older farmers die, knowledge of farming takes a serious loss with their passing. Seldom have decision making responsibilities passed on to the succeeding generation in a timely manner. The learning curve for the next generation of farmers who may step up in their place can be difficult and expensive.

Do you think I am describing myself? Yes, this is my home and my life. I have no desire to change that. But I am thinking of the buffalo. Yes, they will be in good hands when I am gone, I see to that. What I am lacking is the resources and ability to do more right here to expand the herd, so I look elsewhere. I want to see that One Million Buffalo.

The One Million Buffalo campaign touches my heart. I believe that would be a wonderful thing for the buffalo, for people and for our environment – and it would be just incredible to see that happen. For the campaign to be successful, both new farmers AND new consumers are needed.

Buffalo have a special appeal to people, from history, their magnificent presence, or simply love for the animal. People who never thought of farming or ranching entertain the idea of having buffalo in their lives and it becomes very appealing. There is no age limitations, it affects the young, the old and everyone in between. Leon and I fell into this group, with no experience at all with livestock.

Raising buffalo can also be appealing to those who already have livestock, and the first thing we tell them is to forget what they know about cattle, as buffalo are different. So they compare the unknown to what they already know. Its difficult to make a good decision that way but the market for bison is appealing to them as are the animals. If they experiment with raising bison and get reasonable mentoring on the animals it soon becomes a bison ranch and commodity cattle are left behind.

I believe that the bison community is a very special place. Folks generously help new people and welcome them as friends. There is very little competition, rather a sense of co-operation and comradeship. Finding someone to mentor the startup of a new bison operation is easy and an important step in starting a new bison farm.

There are no shortage of young people who want to get into agriculture in general. They seldom hear of raising bison in schools, its not a common curriculum. It takes time for new farms to become profitable and costs involved are a high hurdle to get past. An off farm job is usually required which means living in a non rural area. Land is more expensive there and equipment and livestock require an investment that is often beyond their means. But with help from family, friends and community, its not impossible. Its a pleasure to welcome these young folks into our bison community.

I am continually amazed to see the ingenuity the young people bring to the farm. Three of the young farms in our bison organization use the farm for weddings and other venues to bring more income to the farm. Older folks tend to be more into giving paid tours of their farms. Meat sales bring added revenue and breeding stock sales are always at the core. Overlooked often is the great value of land equity, unrealized until a sale of property is required. In the meantime, the land equity is the enjoyment of living in the farming environment with these wonderful buffalo.

I take great pleasure in helping new farmers start a buffalo herd. And I don't discriminate based on age. Older folks who want to take that step are just as deserving of the experience as the younger folks. Remember that Leon was seventy before we got our first buffalo and that was twenty two years ago. The senior's expectations are usually different. Often they just want to enjoy a few animals rather than making this a farming endeavor. They. provide wonderful homes for their bison and the bison provide countless hours of pleasure for their owners.

Young people look toward the future with dreams in their eyes. What they lack in experience, they make up for with energy and ideas. And they can and do learn, just let them get involved and get the chance. They are the future of the bison industry and we need to nurture and mentor them for success. Come on One Million Buffalo!

I view my responsibility to the One Million Bison campaign to be mentor to new bison producers. And I LOVE my job. Needless to say, talking to folks about buffalo is my favorite conversation. My friends say that my face lights up when I talk buffalo – I know my heart does. Phone calls come in asking for my thoughts on ideas and issues raising bison and that person can tell its a pleasure not an imposition for me to talk to them.

Many calls come from my website and the people are too far away to visit with personally. But that does not mean that I can't give them meaningful help with their dreams. They are always invited to visit and many do so. You can bet they will be hooked on the idea of raising bison by the time they leave my farm. It does not always work out in their life at the time, but the dream will stay with them and someday may become a reality.

Many states have a bison organization with folks who are more than ready to help new bison folks. If there is not one, just look for a neighboring state association. Officers of the organization are a good place to start asking questions and they can refer you to someone who is most likely to be able to help. Half of the Missouri membership lives in other states, so you may find someone close to you on a neighboring state's membership list. Visiting as many farms as possible is the very best way to learn.

Selling heifers to start a new herd is a good thing for me. I know they will have good lives and be well cared for. But you know I hate to see them leave...... As I write this, a new babe was born last night. I don't know if its a boy or girl yet. Its so tiny and new that its a miracle to see it standing to suckle milk and follow its mother as she leads it away. One more bison babe in the world fills my heart with happiness and pride.

I've come up with a way to keep my bison heifers by partnering with a friend. We're both pretty pleased with the plan. Rather than selling the heifer calves, I retain them by sending them to my friend Joe's farm. He has the land and only a few bison, so is pleased to add these girls to his herd. I get to visit with them and help with plans to care for them. He gets my experience and a larger herd without added investment. We will share the offspring of that herd.

Can you imagine? Rather than a one time profit, these girls will still be mine – and Joe's – and I will get half the babes from them for years to come, likely a forty percent return each year on the investment just for deferring profit. I don't know anywhere you could get that kind of return. Joe gets the same return without the upfront investment and has little costs in caring for them. Since the work is pleasure, it is both a cost and a benefit. Time will tell if the experiment will work, but we both have high hopes for our joint herd.

Having a joint herd has other good things about it as well. I have the sole responsibility for my herd here at home. It is a pleasure to share responsibilities with a friend. We hope the herd grows bigger and better each year. So far we have nine shared girls and look forward to adding that many again this year from my herd.

When our joint herd has reached its optimal capacity, I'll be looking around for another friend who wants to share a joint herd. I can visualize herds all over the place with my heifer babes as the core. Yup, I can definitely help with the campaign for One Million Buffalo in the world. I'll be busy for that next twenty two years. Looks like I have dreams in my eyes as well. Buffalo will do that for you.

Are you still here with me? Bless your heart if you have read this far, you just might like buffalo a lot too. Do I have you enthused about the One Million Buffalo campaign as well? Remember that you are an important partner in that campaign. We can't reach the goal without your help. As a consumer, you give the economic value to these animals so that we can afford to raise them. Its just a fact of life that we have to eat buffalo to save them. As you enjoy that taste bison burger or steak, you will know that

you are helping to restore our national mammal to its natural home and dominion in this world.

This story is not over, its alive and growing. My only regret with the book was that I could not print it in color without it becoming cost prohibitive. And there were so many beautiful pictures I wish you could see in color. Many are on my website at www.ourbufalofarm.com, and even better, there is a link on the homepage to facebook. Or you could go directly to facebook at www.facebook.com/carol.klein.988 There you can keep up with what is going on at the farm and see not only the color pictures, but videos as well. I hope you have now become one of those friends I haven't met yet. Please do come and visit on line or on farm.

I've enjoyed telling you my stories about the buffalo and hope you have found them interesting. I'd be grateful if you could take the time to review this book on Amazon. It only takes a minute and would be really helpful in getting this story to others. I'm hoping Buffalo Children will be another step to restoring One Million Buffalo. Thank you friend and I hope our paths will cross again on the Buffalo Trail.
Carol Klein